Imagine Such a Life

Imagine Such a Life

*Stories from
Boston's Most
Enduring
Neighborhoods*

VOLUME IV

Allston-Brighton, Roslindale,
South End, West Roxbury

 CITY OF BOSTON   GRUBSTREET, INC.

With special thanks to all of the participants
for making this book possible

OFFICE OF THE MAYOR
Thomas M. Menino, Mayor
Michael Kineavy, Chief of Policy and Planning

COMMISSION ON AFFAIRS OF THE ELDERLY,
    CITY OF BOSTON
Emily K. Shea, Commissioner
Tula Mahl, Deputy Commissioner
Eileen O'Connor, Staff Photographer
Greg Josselyn, Staff Assistant

GRUBSTREET, INC.
Eve Bridburg, Founder and Executive Director
Christopher Castellani, Artistic Director
Whitney Scharer, Director of Development
    and Communications
Sonya Larson, Program Director
Chip Cheek, Head Instructor
Sean Van Deuren, Volunteer Coordinator
Alison Murphy, Program Manager
Lauren Rheaume, Registrar
Amy Burghardt Muehlbauer, Finance and
    Operations Manager
Drew Arnold, Development Associate

THE MEMOIR PROJECT
Michelle Seaton, Head Instructor and Editor
Kerrie Kemperman, Project Manager, Series
    Editor, and Head Writing Coach
L. Soul Brown, Carrie Normand, Kathleen Olesky,
    and Julie Wittes Schlack, Writing Coaches
Alexis Rizzuto, Advisor
Julia Boyles, Copyeditor and Book Designer
Mark R. Robinson, Cover Designer
Todd Gieg, Photographer

CONTRIBUTORS
Amy Ryan, President, Boston Public Library
Millie McLaughlin, Executive Director,
    Veronica B. Smith Senior Center
Deborah L. McPhee, Community Relations
    Director, Edelweiss Village
Sean M. McCarthy, President, Emerald Society
    of Boston
The South End Library
The Harvard Club
Catering by: Emilio's Pizza, 536 Tremont Street;
    Cristelle's Pizza, 5268 Washington Street;
    and Checkmate Café, 902 South Street.

GrubStreet and the *Memoir Project* are enormously
grateful to the following funders for their generous
support: the Llewellyn Foundation, the Boston
Cultural Council, the Massachusetts Cultural
Council, and the National Endowment for the Arts.

Compilation copyright © 2013
City of Boston and GrubStreet, Inc.

All essays and photographs used with permission

ISBN 978-0-615-89684-7
Printed in the United States by Kase Printing, Inc.
10 9 8 7 6 5 4 3 2 1

ONE OF THE REASONS I am so passionate about Boston is its people. And as part of my job I am lucky that I can spend time getting to know them and hearing their stories. That is why this project is so near to my heart, because it is the stories of the people that make our city great. Due to this amazing project, the *Memoir Project*, we can share those very compelling stories that are so rarely known but make such a great impact. I am so proud to be a part of this project, and I dedicate this book to the people that make Boston strong and proud every day.

May their stories live on,

Thomas M. Menino
Mayor of Boston

Contents

Helping

Growing Up and Good Times

Women's Work

Moving Up and Moving On

Unforgettable Characters

Foreword

"Without libraries, what have we?" asked Ray Bradbury. "We have no past and no future." The essays in *Imagine Such a Life*, the fourth volume in the *Memoir Project* anthology series, bring readers back to a Boston most of us have never experienced and serve as prologue to a future we can only envision. The first three editions of this series — *Born Before Plastic* (2007), *My Legacy Is Simply This* (2008), and *Sometimes They Sang With Us* (2010) — are themselves a library that readers of all ages have enjoyed, learned from, and shared over the past six years. In this new collection, GrubStreet and the City of Boston again offer stories from seniors in four new neighborhoods: Allston-Brighton, Roslindale, the South End, and West Roxbury. These short works, along with the accompanying set of photographs, paint a compelling and intimate portrait of the times, places, and people that have shaped our city. In many ways, the authors in this volume have also authored the story of Boston.

Participants began writing their essays during the four-week memoir workshop led by GrubStreet instructor Michelle Seaton. They then spent another four weeks revising a single essay, and working one-on-one with a GrubStreet writing coach from a team of dedicated mentors led by Kerrie Kemperman. In both the coaching and the small-group class, GrubStreet stressed the importance of honesty in memoir as the authors revisited difficult and pleasant experiences alike. Throughout, they all reminded each other of the beauty of documenting the details of one's life in order to preserve them for future generations.

The *Memoir Project* began in the summer of 2005, when Mayor Thomas M. Menino and GrubStreet joined forces to design a free program for seniors that met the needs of both organizations. GrubStreet wanted to expand its writing classes to teach underserved populations the craft of memoir, and the City of Boston wanted to provide seniors free programs that were rich in quality beyond traditional health and human services. In particular, Mayor Menino recognized a compelling need to enable older residents of the city to give voice to their thoughts and feelings by putting meaningful events from their lives on paper. Our first workshops were held in the North End, Roxbury, and South Boston; the second group was held in Charlestown, Chinatown, East Boston, and Mattapan; and the third in Hyde Park, Jamaica Plain, and Mission Hill. These classes and the ensuing anthologies also inspired the Nantucket Writers Studio to work with GrubStreet on a workshop and anthology of its own in 2010–2011. For our Boston workshops, the City of Boston Elderly Commission ensured that every senior who signed up was able to attend the workshops and coaching sessions, found wonderful classroom spaces at community centers, and arranged for delicious lunches from local caterers.

Over the past eight years, seniors from the fourteen neighborhoods we have visited have read their work on American Public Radio, at the Boston Public Library, Borders Bookstore, the South Boston Public Library, CCTV, the Harvard Club, and at various elementary, middle, and high schools across the city. Many participants have been inspired to continue writing, take additional writing workshops, and even publish.

All four essay collections in this series document the ordinary and extraordinary lives of Bostonians who are our neighbors, friends, and families. We hope this trip back to the old neighborhoods with these new authors prompts you to look at our city in a new light, and maybe even inspires you to record some of your own history.

CHRISTOPHER CASTELLANI
Artistic Director, GrubStreet

MAYOR THOMAS M. MENINO
City of Boston

EVE BRIDBERG
Founder and Executive Director, GrubStreet

EMILY K. SHEA
Commissioner on Affairs of the Elderly

Introduction

"I DON'T KNOW WHERE TO BEGIN to describe what it was like living in a tenement in the 1940s to teenagers who can't imagine such a life," wrote Marion Fennell Connolly in her essay "Life in a Tenement" (page 57). A fundamental goal of the *Memoir Project* is to encourage readers of all ages to indeed "imagine such a life," and so, with thanks to Marion, that became the title of this volume.

There has been a generational shift in participants since our first *Memoir Project* classes in the summer of 2006. At that time, many of the writers belonged to what is sometimes called the Greatest Generation, those old enough to remember the Great Depression and to have worked or served during World War II. Their stories described sacrifice and tenacity in the face of great struggle. Sometimes they didn't want to write about themselves at all. This was the case with Mary O'Keefe, who was the life of the West Roxbury classroom and who passed away before this volume was published. She didn't want to chronicle her own story because she felt that her maternal grandfather, boxing writer Dan Saunders, was far more interesting. This volume is dedicated to her.

Lately, most of our participants have been part of the Silent Generation or the Lucky Few—those born between 1925 and 1942. They were children during World War II, and they remember well the ration cards, but they also remember falling in love and starting a family during the peace that followed. They recall medical advances and economic boom times. Their stories often celebrate the sacrifices of their parents, the beauty of lifelong friendships, the innocence of teenage adventure, and the stability of their families even during difficult times.

Now we hear from the next generation, the Baby Boomers, men and women born after 1945 who came of age in the 1960s. They tell stories of challenging authority and striving for social justice.

In every classroom, we now have a mixture of three generations of elders—people who may be separated in age by thirty years and therefore are not contemporaries in any way—yet the spirit of open sharing has not wavered. In Brighton, a participant read aloud from his journal about mourning his older brother who went away to war and never returned. Another participant read about her struggle to come out to her ailing mother. Listeners wiped away tears and thanked the writers for their work and their vulnerability. This is the power of memoir. Writing about our lives invites others to feel what we once felt. It requires us to truly empathize with others as well as with our own past selves.

No project of this scope can persist without a corps of supporters. Mayor Thomas Menino's vision helped shape this project from its earliest days. Tula Mahl, Deputy Commissioner of the Boston Commission of Elderly Affairs, found venues and promoted the classes. Her colleague, Gregory Josselyn, assisted in each classroom. Our writing coaches—L. Soul Brown, Carrie Normand, Kathleen Olesky, and Julie Wittes Schlack—joined us in working one-on-one with participants. Christopher Castellani, Artistic Director of GrubStreet, has supported this project since the very first workshop. Our beautiful books are thanks to our creative team: Julia Boyles, Todd Gieg, and Mark Robinson. Numerous others keep this project going.

With the publication of this volume, the *Memoir Project* moves on to new neighborhoods in Boston, as it must, because there are more stories to tell, more friends to meet.

MICHELLE SEATON
Head Instructor & Editor

KERRIE KEMPERMAN
Writing Coach & Series Editor

True Loves

YES: A STORY OF LOVE

Mary A. McCarthy

I was fifty-five years old and living upstairs from my ninety-two-year-old mother, helping to care for her and the house — not that she needed much care. She was still driving to her senior luncheon and card games daily, but she could not live on her own anymore. I had made a commitment to myself to stay with her. I had accepted that I would be single until she died, and there were few signs of that happening anytime soon. She was active and vital, and I was content with my choice.

One afternoon while working on a house project with my dear friend Ginny, we took a break to sit in the sun. She asked directly, "I hope you're not waiting until your mother dies." But I was. She continued, "What if your lover never got to meet your mom, who is so important in your life? Or your mom never got to meet the girl of your dreams?" My heart thumped inside my chest. It almost hurt. My heart had opened. I knew it.

3

Then along came Liz, and she is more than I could ever have dreamed.

On our first date on a Sunday morning, Liz and I were sitting on the front porch. My mother passed by on her way to church. As I introduced her to Liz, my mother said quite clearly, "I know you." And off she went. Obviously, in her heart my mother had recognized Liz even though this was their first introduction. Liz and I spent the rest of the day getting to know one another.

We had been going out together only a short while when we realized and accepted how very comfortable we were with one another, how easy it was to enjoy each other, and how much we longed to be together. It was my mother's suggestion that I might want to consider living with Liz. So she moved in.

Liz and I wove together a lovely home for ourselves. We enjoyed working on projects together. We visited each other's favorite spots and talked about every imaginable subject. Liz wrote and read poetry to me. Together we cared for my mother.

During my mother's last two weeks, as she was dying, she said to me, "Oh, isn't Liz so wonderful? She's the best decision we've ever made."

One year to the day after Liz and I met, my mother died.

∽

During the *Memoir Project* class at the Senior Center in Brighton, I read this journal entry aloud. When I finished, I closed my black marbled notebook. My heart was in my hands. I looked around the table. All was a blur. Then, Ita, who was sitting beside me, looked into my eyes and said, "Oh, Mary, wasn't your mother a wise woman?"

Yes.

AN ENDURING LOVE

Sheba (Brown) Barboza

For me, it was love at first sight. I was jumping rope with my cousin and the other neighbor girls, and noticed a boy walking down Haskins Street. When he hit the top of the hill, Bonnie said, "Oh, here comes my cousin, Dougie." My family had just moved to Boston from Charlottesville, Virginia. It was the summer of 1950, and I was fourteen years old. We were living in my aunt's home on Haskins Street in Roxbury.

My sisters were both older than me, by two and three years. Mom would often tell us, "If you get too close to these boys, things happen and you end up pregnant—like so-and-so down in Virginia." She was ever vigilant. None of my friends had phones at home. We didn't either, so Mom had to rely on the fact that we would pay attention to what she said, that boys and girls and sex was a serious situation. I suddenly felt something for Dougie, and thought, "This was what mom was talking about." I was kind of scared.

Bonnie was Dougie's cousin. She must have introduced us that first time, but because of my mother's lectures, I was more afraid of him than shy. I never spoke to him except to say hi. Then it would be over until the next time he started down my street. I would be jumping rope with my cousin and his cousin, and someone would say, "Here comes Dougie," and I would just disappear. My cousin Pat knew. Bonnie knew. Everybody knew. She must have told him at some point, "Sheba likes you."

We never even talked. I wouldn't have let him get near me if he'd tried. But I don't think Dougie Fairhurst thought about me at all once he walked on by because usually he was on his way to the park, and there were more mature girls there. Yes, I was jumping rope until he showed up. My mother knew about that park, and I knew I wasn't to hang out there.

After we moved out of my aunt's house to our own house on Sterling Street, I didn't see Dougie anymore, and I stopped thinking about him. I attended Girls' High School and never had a boyfriend in my four years there. I think the fact that there were no boys in school was the main reason why, but they were always hanging around outside the school when we got out. When a boy asked me out, I would say, "Can I bring my girlfriend?" and then I wouldn't hear from him again. Why did I think he had the money to take out both me and a girlfriend?

It wasn't until after I graduated from high school that I had my first boyfriend. I was in the church choir, and one day the organist brought a friend, Stanley, to rehearsal. My mom wasn't happy because Stanley was four years older than me and had been in the army. He had served in the Korean War. He had been around. We married anyway. We were together four years and had a son, Stanley, Jr., before we divorced in 1963.

In 1998, forty-eight years after our first meeting on Haskins Street, Dougie was taking pictures at his cousin's wedding, and one of my sisters-in-law was there. They got to talking about the old neighborhood and Haskins Street, and she happened to mention my name. Dougie said, "Oh, my God, Sheba Brown. Where is my girl?" She wouldn't tell him much, so he asked for my phone number. She insisted that Dougie give her his number instead and said she would pass it on to me. He gave her three numbers: home, beeper, and cell. Now, I'm still cautious about these men because they'll give you their home number and there's a wife answering the phone. I've got three phone numbers for Dougie and I don't know where to call; I didn't know what a beeper was. I called his home and a woman answered, so I still don't know anything. When Dougie got on the phone, I said, "Hi Dougie. This is Sheba." We talked, and Dougie explained that it was his mother who had answered. He had lived with her in Hingham since his father passed away. He was going to Detroit for the weekend, but we made a date to talk after he got back. I called my sister-in-law to tell her. Now I'm all nervous; I'm going to meet this good-looking boy I used to know. I'm older; I'm ready for anything now.

"What do you look like?" I had asked him. "Oh, yeah, I'm about the same," he said. No, he was not the same. When I went down there and answered the door, it was Dougie — but with a big belly. Now I'm mad as hell at my sister-in-law, because she didn't say anything about Dougie being fat! We had a nice conversation, though.

Dougie and Sheba

We laughed about Haskins Street, and how I wouldn't let him anywhere near me. He reminded me that we had seen one another once at a station when I was working for the MBTA. I remember yelling, "Dougieeeeee!" But he hadn't tracked me down afterward, and that had been many years ago. He had worked at Northeastern University and had retired recently. He had married twice and had four children. I guess I let him come back a week or so later, and he took me out to eat in Dedham. And that starts the saga of Douglas Fairhurst and Sheba (Brown) Barboza.

We spent weekends visiting family and just having lots of laughs. Whenever we were with my family, Dougie would tell my brothers, "Your sister wouldn't even let me sit on her front steps!" That made everyone laugh. My brothers would say, "Doug, we don't believe you. That is not true!"

Dougie loved to drive, and we traveled to New York, Virginia, Georgia, Detroit, Texas, Rhode Island, New Hampshire, and Maine. It was comical — wherever we traveled, his deep voice and thick Boston accent got noticed. Even in restaurants along the road, people would comment. We went everywhere in his Cadillac. Oh, how I loved to see his car drive up to my door. Even though he had retired, he worked a newspaper route in Hingham to pay for his gorgeous car. The Hingham area wasn't an easy delivery route. The paper had to be dropped off at the door — up long, unpaved, snowy driveways. But he didn't complain; he said he just wished it didn't have to be happening at that time in our lives. Coincidentally, we had both retired in 1998. He used to tell me, "We'll be driving down I-95 South in another year, Sheeb."

In early June 2011, Dougie had a cough that would not go away. He had visited his new primary care doctor, but she didn't see any problems and didn't prescribe anything. Yet the cough persisted. Finally, I said, "Dougie, I don't like how that cough sounds. Please stop by the hospital and get checked again." He said, "No, Sheeb, you know they will keep me all day, and I need to get home and rest for work." His deliveries started at 11:00 PM, but he promised he would go the next morning after he finished at 8:00. I arrived home around 3:00 in the afternoon. He hadn't called. I called his cell and home phones. No response. I called the emergency room at Boston Medical Center to find that he was there and was being admitted. When he arrived to his room, I was there waiting. He came in on a stretcher. "Sheeb, what are you doing here?" This is the way he greeted everybody—at a party, dance, wake, anything.

The nurse said, "Douglas has pneumonia. He'll be out in a couple of days." I breathed a sigh of relief—*two days, that's nothing*. The staff let me stay after visiting hours, until nine or ten o'clock at night. I kept kissing him. I wouldn't let him rest. "Sheeb, stop kissing me. I've got pneumonia. You'll catch it!" I laughed and told him that I would not. The nurse confirmed that I wouldn't catch his pneumonia.

The second day when I visited he seemed okay. His cough wasn't so bad. The medical staff was running tests, and he was told to stay in bed. I stayed overnight and left the next morning to go home and change. His family was visiting with him. Dougie said, "See you later, Sheeb," and we kissed. He always said, "Thanks, Sheeb." He never failed to say thanks. Sometime that day he was moved to intensive care because he couldn't breathe, and he needed to be put on oxygen. I was so upset going up that elevator. Meanwhile, he was very hungry and upset. He hadn't been allowed any food or drink, and he was angry with the nurses. It was very upsetting to all of us, but none of us realized that he was becoming more ill. The doctors planned to put a breathing tube down his throat that day.

I thought, *Okay, just another procedure*. Dougie and I hugged, kissed. When I came back a couple of hours later, the tube had been installed and the machine was doing the breathing. What a horrible sight. It sounded like the drilling out on the street. Dougie was unconscious. I cried, "What happened to my Dougie? Is he going to wake up or speak to me again?" I would whisper in his ear, "Dougie, I'm sorry you're sick, babe. You're going to be okay. You're here at Boston Medical Center. They are the best. You're going to be fine." He must have been dying then.

That third morning when he had said, "See you later," was the last I saw of my Dougie alive. His eyes never opened again. His blood pressure had dropped and the doctors couldn't get it to rise. His kidneys failed. Continuous dialysis was administered. Nothing worked. This went on for two more days until his heart failed.

I was at the home of one of my brothers when I found out that Dougie had passed. My cousin called with the sad news. I had talked to some of Dougie's family about having him buried in Boston because I wanted to be able to visit him. Well, I guess that fell on deaf ears; they had him cremated. One of my brothers attended the service and my nephew did, as well. I did not. Now I place objects for Dougie on my mother's and sister's gravestone. It gives me something to focus on while I pray.

God gave Dougie to me for thirteen great years — 1998 to 2011 — and then took him away. I was so dependent on him; I hadn't realized how much. I came to love both his belly and him completely. Often I still think to myself, *Oh, I'll call Dougie and tell him.* A few months before he passed, Dougie's answering machine had changed from his voice to an automated voice. If his voice had still been on that answering machine, I might have had an opportunity to record it.

Dougie, you are in my every thought and movement. Oh, how you took care of me. Thank you, Dougie.

HOW THE RED SOX
CAPTURED MY HEART

Anne Mahoney

My father loved baseball and I came to love the game, as well, through a lucky chance. Neither of my two brothers was a particularly good ball player nor very interested in the game even though Dad loved it. When the neighborhood kids played pickup ball games, I was one of the girls who played. These games included both boys and girls, and none of us were skillful players. I think I got picked because I truly loved baseball and understood enough of the rules that I had an idea of what I was doing. This was long before there was Little League or any softball teams for girls — at least in Brighton.

My love affair with the game began in the summer of 1948 when I was nine, and my father was on his two-week vacation from the Boston Elevated Railway Company, which is now the MBTA. Dad was going to take my two brothers, who were then seven and eight years old, to a Red Sox game, but one of them got sick and the other was being punished for something or other, so he decided to take me. It was a treat to be going somewhere alone with my father. Occasionally, I had gone shopping in Boston with just my mother, but I don't remember ever having gone somewhere alone with my father. We took the streetcar to Kenmore and then walked to Fenway Park on a warm summer afternoon. At that time, most games were afternoon games. Dad explained the game to me and — when I had a question — some of its finer points. I don't remember if the Red Sox won, but I'm pretty sure they did since I fell in love with the team. I don't think I would have been so impressed if they had lost that day to the St. Louis Browns, which even *I* knew was not a good team.

One memory I have is of this loud, heavy man wearing shirtsleeves with suspenders and a straw hat, sitting rather near us and yelling at one of the players, Wally Moses. I was amazed at this grown-up yelling like that, and I spent quite a bit of time staring at him. We were seated in the left-field grandstand about halfway between third base and the left-field corner, and he was to the left of us. I can still see him yelling at Wally Moses — that he was a bum. Wow! He wasn't swearing or anything like that, just calling Wally a name, something that kids might do if there were no grown-ups around, but certainly not any adults that I knew. For some reason, Ted Williams didn't play that day, and Wally was playing left field in his place. Maybe that's why this gentleman was giving poor Wally the business. I developed a crush on the second baseman, Bobby Doerr, whom I continued to follow until his retirement. Whenever he came up at a crucial time during a game that I was listening to on the radio or — years later — watching on TV, I would say a quick Hail Mary for him to get a hit.

I don't go to many games now, but I do follow the Red Sox fortunes pretty closely. I recently read *The Teammates* by David Halberstam about the friendship among Dom DiMaggio, Johnny Pesky, Bobby Doerr, and Ted Williams that lasted for over sixty years until Ted Williams died. All of these men played that day, except Ted, and I followed them for years. I enjoyed that book because I had followed the players for a long time. I think Bobby Doerr is still alive.

A couple of days after my first Red Sox game, my mother and father went to another baseball game — a night game with the Boston Braves down at Braves Field. Because I was now officially in love with baseball and a big Red Sox fan, they took me as well. Again, it was just my mother and father and me — no brothers or sisters along. I can still see it, a warm summer night sitting in the right-field bleachers of Braves Field (now Boston University's Nickerson Field). We were way, way back, but this park wasn't as big as Fenway, and I remember looking out of the park into the night where you could see the road and the lights from the seats. It is in the area where the Mass Turnpike is now, and I have to admit I was as interested in looking around as I was in watching the game. I don't remember anyone yelling at anyone or if the Braves won or not. They probably did; they won the National League pennant that year. It didn't matter. The Red Sox had captured my heart.

I can also remember going to games at Fenway Park when I was in the eighth grade, and my Catholic school got out for early release time when the Catholic kids from the public school came for religious instruction. More than once, a couple of friends and I took the streetcar to Kenmore and sat in the bleachers behind the bullpen

Red Sox girl with her Dad

watching and sometimes talking to the relief pitchers. We thought we were really cool. Some forty years later I met a friend who said she did the same thing, but she came over from Mission Hill. How times have changed.

One morning in 1986, out of the blue, my boss gave me tickets to game two of the Red Sox/California Angels American League Championship Series. I surprised my father by calling him and asking if he'd like to go. He was shocked that I had the tickets and almost giddy with the excitement of seeing a championship game.

Once again, my dad and I headed off to Fenway Park together. This time we took the bus, as the streetcar was no longer running. It was a perfect October afternoon, bright and sunny. We had box seats behind home plate and were surrounded by businessmen. This time I know the Red Sox won. Unfortunately, that was the year of Bill Buckner's horrible error, but, for that October day, we were as happy as two Red Sox fans could be. I think that championship game was probably the last game Dad saw in person, but he had a few more years to suffer with them on TV.

BROWN-EYED GIRL

Nancy O'Hara

May 14, 1990. We had been pacing the floor for twenty minutes. It was a little after 6:00 PM on the day after Mother's Day, and we were about to meet our little Marlene outside the elevator on the second floor of the Santiago Sheraton. The attorney and his secretary were delivering her to us. They were late, because a crowd of Chilean teenyboppers was milling around the driveway hoping to see a Brazilian musical sensation who was also staying at the Sheraton. Our anxiety level was high, and I was filled with many apprehensions.

The door opened, and there stood this forlorn little two-and-a-half-year-old brown-eyed girl. For me, it was the moment of birth and the start of our new life together. I lost my composure and sobbed as I gathered this frightened girl to me. After all these years and longing, here she was. Her new papa and new brother, Mike, age eight, were excited participants.

We all went back to our suite. The attorney introduced us to Marlene as Papa and Mama, and she crawled into our laps and called us by our names. It was here that Mike showed his true colors. Although he wasn't ecstatic about the whole idea, he was touched by Marlene and started to play with her and show her the presents he had brought for her. In fact, the secretary, after just six minutes, clapped her hands and said, *"Finito!"* She saw that the adjustment was satisfactory. But we were having such a good time that we opened a bottle of champagne, and they stayed for an hour.

Marlene slept like an angel in a crib in her brother Mike's room and was content as long as she had her pacifier. I had a fitful night. At 5:00 AM I tiptoed in, and there she was, awake in her crib with an apprehensive look. She saw me, and her countenance turned to wonder, then puzzlement, then amazement. I was oblivious to the fact that my hair was rolled in green plastic rollers, but I must have looked like a space alien. I scooped her up and took her into the big bed to cuddle and there we played with the bag of rollers. Then I began to roll her hair. We laughed and played until about 9:00 AM when her brother and father began to awaken.

Each day we spent with Marlene she became more comfortable with us. She had been in a foster home for a few months. She did not know how to kiss or hug. Mike nicknamed her "Mrs. Clean" because she loved taking baths and shampooing her hair. She loved to use a napkin to wipe her mouth. Her bathroom hygiene was impeccable, and she was fully toilet trained. She'd say, *"El baño,"* and trot off to the bathroom.

We decided that Marlene must have thought the beautiful hotel was home. Each time we returned to the marble lobby with its huge floral arrangements and a glass wall looking out to a beautiful pool, garden, and children's playground, Marlene would stand there and say, *"Mi casa!"*

We didn't know if she thought we were just another foster family, but on the night we flew out of Chile I think it began to sink in that she was really ours. I sensed she knew something important was happening. She kept saying, *"El avión, el avión!"* (the plane, the plane). We boarded and within a couple of hours, she was in dreamland, and she slept the rest of the trip. Marlene arrived in Miami pretty refreshed, but I was wiped out because I had been holding her all night. It must have been a need of mine to hold her, as she had her own seat.

We arrived back in Boston at 3:30 PM, and Mike had a Little League game at five o'clock. We bundled Marlene up and took her down to the park to watch the game. Our son got his very first hit of the season and got four men out at third base. This was very good for his ego, as there was lots of attention on Marlene. She was so social and happy, and started playing with some other toddlers. She was chattering a mile a minute in Spanish, but none of the children seemed to notice.

During our first week home, we had a steady stream of visitors. Relatives, friends, and neighbors took turns coming to welcome Marlene, our beautiful daughter. It took her just five minutes or so to warm up, and then she would put on the charm. At night she slept in Mike's old crib and cuddled with her favorite white *"osito"* (teddy bear). Our days were action-packed as we moved back into the busy schedule that was normal for us. Marlene would just go with the flow as long as she got a two- or three-hour nap. From the beginning she showed her *joie de vivre* — rushing to greet her big brother when he came in from school, delighting us with her use of a new word she had heard. We'd all laugh as we caught her in the nick of time as she tried to squeeze Ivory dishwashing liquid onto her broccoli and cheese.

Within two weeks it seemed as though Marlene had been with us from birth.

~

Flash forward twenty years to August 2010. Marlene was now twenty-two years old and had, by most people's standards, a great life.

She had always had access to her adoption file so she had always known the full, four-part name of her mother. One day at work, she typed those four names into the computer, and *voilá!* There was her biological mother, listed with an address including the number, street, and town in Chile. Using Google Maps, Marlene could actually see the building her birth mom lived in.

Marlene decided to write a letter and see if this was in fact her birth mother. With the help of her boyfriend Henry, who was fluent in Spanish, she composed a letter using Henry's family home in Jamaica Plain as the return address. Marlene mailed her inquiry and explained that she has had a wonderful life in the U.S. She wanted her birth mother to know that she'd graduated from college, was enjoying her job, and was happy and healthy.

Marlene and Nancy, 1990

The letter arrived in Chile. Marlene's half brother, Miguel, age 20, lived at home at the time, and read the letter postmarked Boston, as well. (Marlene is the only person we know with two brothers both named Mike.) Miguel promptly began to search on the Internet and Facebook for someone named Henry S. from Jamaica Plain, and sure enough he discovered Henry's Facebook page and wrote to him, asking if he knew someone named Marlene.

Now what was Marlene going to do?

That very night we had supper together and afterward my husband suggested that we all go to the living room for a family chat. This had never happened before, so I was bewildered. He had heard Marlene's story on the ride home from work that evening, and she had been very upset, fearing that we might be hurt by her search for her birth mother. We settled in on the sofa and chairs, and Marlene revealed what had happened. I saw that she was overcome with emotion. She did not want us distressed by her Internet searching. Her eyes filled as she assured us we had given her a great life. I knew I had just a few seconds to react. My initial response was, "Oh Marlene, this is great news — that is just what I would have done if I had access to these search engines." I could sense her relief.

My mind flashed back twenty years to the original phone call telling us of a little toddler in Santiago needing a home. There had been three months between the phone call and the plane ride to Chile, and I remember spending a lot of time thinking about her mother and what a heartbreaking choice she was making. I had grieved for her then.

Now my thoughts were on Marlene, caught up in her emotional turmoil. I was thinking Marlene had done a good thing. Her mother would now know that she had given Marlene life twice — at her birth and again in her release. Now her birth mother would know that her little daughter had grown up, survived, and blossomed, that she was happy and healthy, thinking of her and her sacrifice, and grateful. Marlene knew that her birth mom had put her child's well-being first.

We awaited her birth mother's reply. Within a week, Marlene received a letter from Chile. She showed us the short note written in beautiful cursive on lovely stationery, but we could not understand the Spanish. I offered to translate it via Babelfish.com, one of those amazing sites on the Internet, but Marlene declined my offer.

Now, eight months later, I remain curious — but patient. In due time, Marlene may share the translated contents of the letter. In the meantime, I often wonder what I would have said if the roles were reversed. I imagine that I might have written, "Thank you, dear Marlene, for understanding that I had good reasons for making this difficult choice, and I thank you for sharing with me how your life has turned out, how you were loved and given a chance to live a healthy life, and to be all that you can be. I am happy that you were cared for by a loving and nurturing family."

A LOVE OF MUSIC

Gail Jacobs

Every Sunday morning, I would sit in the living room with my father and enjoy a recording from his vast classical collection. He always sat in his chair, and I would sit close by on the sofa. I remember that the furniture was comfortable. He would close his eyes while he listened. He must have needed that time to relax. I used to relax with him even though at that age I didn't have any stress. I was probably five years old.

As young as I was, the beautiful classical music moved me. Some pieces had such soaring and thunderous notes, while the next moment could be quiet and very calming. It roused my emotions even as a child. This was the beginning of my introduction to the music that I have loved all my life.

My father was an electronics engineer, and he worked long hours. Some days during the week, he was away at work so much that I didn't see him. But come Sunday morning, we had our time together. We listened to Tchaikovsky, Rachmaninoff, and Strauss. After a while, other types of music crept into his collection. He listened to semi-classical and honky-tonk and more popular music of that time. I really enjoyed listening to music, and it has played an enormous part in my life to this day.

When I entered junior high school, I started taking violin lessons. I would practice at home — with the bedroom door closed, of course. I really didn't mean to torture my family. After a while I was able to join the school orchestra.

My mother loved music, too, but she was always busy while we listened. She took care of the house, making sure it was immaculate. She was a quiet person, but she definitely made herself well understood. She never wanted anyone to fight; she wanted everyone to enjoy his or her lives, and she frequently reminded us that life was short. My mother always encouraged me to try different things: to play the violin, to do sports, and most of all to keep at things that I found difficult. She wanted me to keep trying, to go beyond what I thought I could do. Because I was a lefty, my first violin teacher thought I wouldn't be able to learn, but it never occurred to me that I couldn't learn. I just did what everybody else was doing. My mother taught me to drive. But most of all, she taught me to cook. It was really not learning, though, because she made it seem like fun. We really had a good time together.

My absolute favorite memory is coming home from school, opening the door to the indescribably delicious aroma of chocolate chip cookies. That was always such a wonderful treat, but afterwards, of course, it was time to do some of my homework and then go out and play or practice the violin.

Our classroom music teacher in junior high was energetic and short, such a dynamo. At that time, the schools offered free music lessons. She brought us together in the school orchestra. She made sure that we played together and stayed together in the music, and even in junior high we sounded good. We were all so different but somehow came together and had a wonderful time. I loved playing music in a group. Not only did I love being with my friends, I loved the way we created music together. Even after high school, lots of us went back often to visit our teacher. She inspired me to continue my love of music.

I relied on that love of music when my mother became ill with leukemia. When she was very sick, my mother said to me, "When you come to visit me in the cemetery, don't be sad. Have a picnic. Think of the good times." By then I was in my thirties and had young children. She loved to have them visit her so she could give them toast with cinnamon, and milk to drink. She stayed happy and encouraged me to do the same. She died in 1974 and it was my first major loss. It was a time of great sadness for me. But the music she encouraged me to love and to play helped me to cope with her death. It still plays a big part in my life.

I had already developed an interest in opera. Even just listening to it took me into such an extraordinary world. I still find the experience of hearing opera beyond description. Many people who love art say that every time they look at a favorite painting they see something new. And that's how I feel about my favorite music. So often, I hear a piece differently from the previous time — whether it's a symphony, an aria, or a popular song—I hear a different emphasis on a phrase or an interpretation of a popular song; it is an awakening for me. I always wonder, "Why didn't I hear that before?" I have had the pleasure of going to Symphony Hall and to Tanglewood in the summer.

A year after my mother died, my husband passed away, as well.

Even when you go through a lot in life, all the trials and troubles, the music is always there for you. No matter what you listen to, even "easy listening" can take you away from your problems. Even those two words—easy listening—just to say the phrase is very calming. My favorites were Pavarotti and Beverly Sills. Even though they are both gone, they still hold a very deep place in my heart.

Like my father, I have surrounded myself with musical recordings. My collection consists of opera, old standards, and Elvis Presley. Just to escape from daily trials and tribulations, I turn to music. It makes me happy and it still transports me to another world.

Struggling Together

I'LL SEE YOU AT MA'S

George McCormack

My clearest recollection of early childhood goes back to the middle 1930s. I remember Mom feeding us all at the kitchen table and wondering where Dad was. Even at the age of five, I knew where he was—at one of the many shops in Allston that served alcoholic beverages. When he finally showed up, supper was over and all he had in his pockets was change. My older brothers would threaten mayhem and Mom would calm them down, and then Dad would disappear for a week or two. This went on for a few years, and when we moved in 1942, Dad was on his own. Mom was a real faithful Catholic and she wouldn't hear of a divorce. I'm sure she conferred with Father McShea.

My dad was an alcoholic and he was dysfunctional. These are two words I probably never heard until I was in my twenties, and yet there is no way I could tell this story without them. It is a mystery to me how I was ever born. How did my mother give birth to seven children? I am the youngest and my oldest brother was fourteen years old when I was born.

My mom instilled a strong work ethic in all of her children, and I watched my older brothers take jobs and leave home. My four oldest brothers all spent time in the Civilian Conservation Corps during the thirties and John, the oldest, joined the army in 1940. Bud, the next oldest, served out in the western part of the state and married a girl in Greenfield in 1937. Mother got her third son, Bob, a job with the local plumbing company in Allston where he worked the rest of his life—with time out for the army, of course. Her fourth son, Joe, enlisted in the navy soon after we settled on Coolidge Road in Allston. Her fifth son, Frank, took a job at Wheeler's, the dry cleaners, on Franklin Street in Allston. The lady who owned the place had asked Mom if she had a grown-up son who could come to work for her. Mom said, "I'm not sure he's fully grown, but he'll be a good worker." She was correct, of course. Frank practically ran the place for the next twenty years—after taking time out to join the navy.

That left Mom with just two children at home to care for. I should mention that she also worked. She left the house every morning to tend to the family of a doctor. She also took care of a few of the doctor's neighbors on Aldie Street and made lunch for some elderly ladies, too. She looked in on a wheelchair-bound lady to make sure she was okay.

As we were growing up, my brothers and I knew we could reap a few coins from these ladies by putting out the barrels or removing storm windows, putting the screens in, and doing a little painting or whatever chores they needed done. Our sister Anne did her share of minding children. They weren't calling it babysitting back then.

Mom oversaw all of this and worried all the time about us, and about money, even though she always told us not to worry over things that we couldn't do anything about. She also had high blood pressure and on many occasions her doctor would open a vein and bleed her. Mom always told us that smoking was no good for us — way ahead of the rest of the world. But when her doctor was trying to get her blood pressure down, he suggested that she should go into the parlor and have a highball and smoke a cigarette. Mom had never drank or smoked in her life, but tried it anyway. We all laughed the first time she let the smoke out her nostrils. She was so proud. A teaspoonful of whiskey in a glass of water was one of the most distasteful things she had ever tried. That was the end of doctor's orders.

One night coming out of church with the group of ladies who were her closest friends, she had what was probably a small stroke and fell, striking her temple on the light pole on the corner. She was incapacitated for a few weeks and the doctor she worked for took her to Florida with the family for a month. She was in good spirits for a long spell.

Mom was a great correspondent. All during World War II she kept in touch with not only all her sons in the services but also with every one of their buddies. The large dining room table always had two or three letters started by Mom on it, and anyone who came up the stairs would be invited and encouraged to write a few lines.

We also had a portable typewriter that always had four or five sheets of carbon paper in it. Mom didn't type, but my sister and I did. Any time one of the guys — my brothers or any of their friends — came home on leave there was a party at our house. They called it

37

"standard procedure." The soldiers would arrive home, hug and kiss their mothers and call their girlfriends, and say, "I'll see you at Ma's." Of course, the Ma they were talking about was Mom. I was at most or all of these homecoming parties. Maybe the greatest one was when Don Stevens brought home twelve of his Marine buddies to be his honor guard when he got married. The young Marines, most of them from down south, stayed at our house overnight and the next morning, Mom marched all of them to church. A couple of the reluctant ones were told by Mom, "Everyone in this house goes to church on Sunday." They were quite a sight in their dress blues.

A few of my brothers' friends had trouble at home, so they came and lived with us until things got better for them. When my brother Frank was in the navy, he was assigned to a new heavy cruiser that was built right here in Massachusetts; while it was getting the finishing touches done, he was able to come home nights. One of his buddies on the ship came from Brooklyn and he could go home only on the weekends. When Mom found out he had a new baby boy, she suggested that he would save a lot of traveling time if his wife and child lived in Boston. That wife and child lived with us for the next six months until they all shipped out of Boston heading for the Pacific.

Mom worried about her five boys in the various services, and it nearly killed her to learn that her first born was killed in action in North Africa on January 28, 1943. My brother John was more of a father to me than our own dad. He was also a true hero and was posthumously awarded a Silver Star for gallantry in action. Poor Mom was never really healthy after that, I guess. Five years later when

George McCormack and Mom

I wanted to enlist in the air force, Mom didn't want me to go. I tried to reassure her that the war was over and I would surely be drafted, and I could choose the schools that suited me best. Mom relented and sent me off with her blessing. I'm sure it didn't help her health about two years later when the Korean "police action" started. My commanding officer at the time was a WWII fighter pilot named Francis M. Groves who liked the way I conducted myself. Major

Groves promoted me twice, so we were pretty good buddies. Once he inquired about my family, and I gave him a short description of things back home. He promptly wrote my mom a letter promising her that I would be home at the end of my hitch and that I wouldn't even be transferred.

I'll never forget that morning I got home. Mom was in bed most of the time as a result of a couple of strokes. When I walked into her bedroom and sat on the bed, we hugged and she held me and wouldn't let me go for a long time, I guess maybe until we both stopped crying.

I had sent her money from every one of my paychecks while I was in the service with the hope that the extra money would help her in some way. I had always given her the money I had earned in my various jobs in childhood. But when I came home, I found that she had put all that money I'd sent into the bank for me. She never spent a dime of it.

Two weeks after I arrived home, I was in the backyard helping Mom hang the wash. The neighbor came out, and Mom introduced us by saying, "My son is looking for work." The next morning I was on the way to Watertown to start my new job, a job that lasted eighteen years.

Even in the last months of her life, Mom was my English teacher, advisor, confidant, music teacher, and best friend. Whenever I was on my way out in the evening, Mom always told me to have a good time, and to behave, and not wait to be entertained, and not to be hesitant if asked to sing along—not that I ever was. Her strokes had left her hands a little trembly, but she sat at the piano and played until I had the songs "Louisville Lou," "Dapper Dan," and "Some Sunny Day" firmly implanted in my brain. Mom passed away in March 1953, less than six months after my discharge from the air force. Not a day goes by that some encounter or something said brings my mom to mind.

My wonderful bride, Mary Lou Carey, whom I married in May 1957, never met her mother-in-law. In my mind, you don't really have memories until you're four years old. That, and the fact that I was away from home for four years in the service, left me with about fifteen years with my mom. Mary Lou's mother also died before we met. She and I had so much in common; maybe that was why we were so perfectly compatible. How incredibly lucky and blessed I was to have two totally wonderful women in my life.

DOLLS AND MY
CHILDHOOD MEMORIES

Delores Hall

My foster grandmother was the only parent I knew. I called her Mama instead of Grandma. She read the Bible a lot and would often quote the verses to me: "Do unto others as you would have them do unto you." She would say, "Give from your heart. Never give someone something that you don't want yourself. You may have a lot or a little to give. When you give, do it quietly." She would frequently ask me, "Do you know you're loved?" and the way she said it, the way she looked at me, always made my eyes tear. When I was six years old, I went with Mama to a small, dimly lit fabric shop. In those days most ladies usually made their own clothes, even coats and hats. While she and a few ladies were looking over the fabric, my eyes wandered around the store. In one corner, I saw a big cardboard box with two doll legs hanging out over the side, and I didn't know if it was a whole or just a half of a doll. I went over and picked up the legs, and I saw it was a whole doll. I was so excited. I had never had a doll before and right away I wanted this one. I ran over to Mama to show her the doll, but she was still busy. When she finally found what she wanted, I asked, "Mama, can I have this doll?" She said yes, and I was so happy. Later, I thought that the doll must have been free so Mama said that I could have it.

The doll did not have any clothes. The head, arms, and legs were made of hard plastic, and her body was stuffed. She was bare just like that. I said to Mama, "My doll needs clothes." She took a small piece of remnant, white with orange stripes, from a box and said, "You can use this piece for a blanket for her." The piece was so small it barely fit around the doll. The next day, Mama began to cut the pattern out for her dress from the fabric she bought. As she cut, pieces of fabric fell to the floor. I picked them up to see if I could put them together to make a pretty dress for my doll, but the pieces were too small.

I was a shy and quiet girl. Mama and my little doll were my only friends. I was happy even if my doll didn't have any clothes. We lived in the same house with another family that had a girl my age; she was my cousin. One afternoon, she and her mother were laughing and playing with her dolls, saying how cute one of them was and how it could stand on its feet. I went out and stood by their door to see the dolls and to hear the fun they were having. They saw me but didn't invite me in. Mama saw me standing there and she whispered, "De, come away from their door. Come back and play with your own doll. You should never worry about what others have. Be thankful for what you have." After seeing my cousin's pretty doll, I didn't want anybody to see my little doll, and I couldn't tell Mama of my feelings.

A few years later, the Sparkle Plenty doll came out. She was a baby doll with long, golden hair that sparkled. She was a character from the comic strip *Dick Tracy*. I asked everybody in the family to buy one for me, but they didn't have enough money. Money was tight at that time. I often saw a pretty doll sitting on my friend's mother's bed whenever I visited, so I dreamed about having a nice doll that I could put on my bed, too. Since every little girl wanted to have a Sparkle Plenty doll, the church had a contest. The girl who sold the most raffle tickets would get a Sparkle Plenty doll as a prize. I walked door-to-door, selling the tickets, but I didn't win the contest, so there was no doll for me, and I was very disappointed.

On my eighth birthday, I woke up to hear Mama say, "De, happy birthday." She gave me a birthday card with the number eight on it. There was a present with the card. It was a pair of brown socks. I was so excited and I ran around to show my card to all the people in the house. I had never gotten a birthday card before. Well, that was the first and last birthday card I had in my childhood.

When I was nine, I remember coming home from school on my birthday. There was a little cake on the table. On the cake, there was a piece of paper cut into the shape of a doll on it. I was so happy, and I laughed and laughed when I hugged Mama.

For my tenth birthday, I expected to see another cake on the table for me, so I told all my classmates that I would have a birthday cake when I got home after school. I ran all the way home. There was no cake on the table. I asked, "Mama, am I going to have a birthday cake?" Mama said, "Honey, you're too old for a birthday cake now." I was ten years old. After that, I never got a birthday cake until I was an adult.

45

SOUTH END

When I was a teenager, I helped make packages of Christmas gifts from the donated stuff for the little kids in Sunday school. I put an apple, an orange, some nuts, and Christmas candy in a brown paper bag. I covered the bag in Christmas wrapping paper and tied it with a piece of ribbon. When I went to the Christmas party at the church, I also got a gift-wrapped present. One year I got a checkerboard game, and my biological grandmother gave me a book called *Black Beauty* and a new snowsuit. I remember that Christmas very well. I didn't see my grandmother regularly. She lived quite far away and she didn't often visit.

On Christmas Eve when I was twelve, Mama needed a new nightgown. She had patched her old one until it was worn out. She gave me two dollars to buy her a flannel nightgown. I went downtown. There were about seven or eight stores on one block and an expensive store, Blumstein's, in the middle of the block. I went into the least-expensive stores, and they were all out of flannel nightgowns. I checked every store, and then went back into each of the stores again even though I knew that all the flannel nightgowns were sold out. I kept passing Blumstein's and I asked myself, "Do I dare go in?" I was so determined that finally I went in. By then there were no other shoppers that late on Christmas Eve. A sales lady came to me and asked, "Young lady, what do you want to buy?" I said, "A flannel nightgown for my grandmother." She took me to the rack. There were a lot of frilly nightgowns and one beautiful flannel one.

"How much does this flannel nightgown cost?" I asked.

"Ten dollars."

I knew I could not afford it. She looked at me and asked kindly, "How much money do you have?"

"Two dollars."

"Can you go home and get more money?" she asked.

I shook my head and walked out of the store because I knew that those two dollars were all the money Mama had.

I left Blumstein's and continued going in and out of the other stores searching for a flannel nightgown. It was getting dark. Finally, I returned to Blumstein's and went to the sales rack and looked at the flannel nightgown again. It was marked two dollars! I bought it. That sales lady offered to wrap it up for me. Years later I realized that the sales lady must have changed the price for me. It was a miracle, a gift, and she sure had the Christmas spirit on that cold night.

Mama's face lit up when I gave her the nightgown. She put it on. At that moment, I thought that she almost looked like a big doll with a new dress on. Mama was so happy she gave me a great big hug, and hugs were few and far in between when I was a child. On that Christmas Eve, Mama had her new nightgown on and she told me, "Kewpie doll," as she sometimes called me, "you are better to me than my own children." I would never forget that Christmas Eve.

When I was fourteen, I got a job after school. I was paid twelve dollars a week. I brought my paycheck home and gave it to Mama. When summer vacation came, I got a summer job. My pay was thirty-five dollars a week, and I brought my pay home and gave Mama all of it. The pay was in a little brown envelope. When I was fifteen, I wanted to buy a skirt and a blouse like my friends had, but

Delores and her doll collection

Mama refused to give me any of the money from my pay and said she was saving the money for my education. So I worked overtime that Saturday to have the money, and I bought the skirt and the blouse. That's when I told myself, "It's time to start sharing my paycheck with me." The next month, I bought myself a doll.

Time went by and it was another Christmastime in the city. I was so happy that I could buy Mama a present with my own money. I bought her another new nightgown. She kept thanking me. I also bought my grandfather a bottle of Canoe cologne that he liked. He put some on and made his funny little sound he would usually make whenever he laughed happily. I was so happy that I could buy gifts for them with my own money.

I never forgot about the dolls. As an adult, I had three daughters. I would make sure that my daughters received beautiful dolls every Christmas. When they got older, they lost interest in playing with dolls. Here was my big chance to make my long-lost dream come true. I collected their old dolls, scattered all over their beds, and turned them into beautiful dolls again with new dresses. I sat them on my own bed. It became a hobby for me to make new dresses for old dolls. I made big rag dolls and I began to buy dolls. My friends and family would bring a doll back for my collection whenever they went on a trip. My son brought me a doll in traditional South American attire from Belize. Now I have dolls from far and near. Today, I have more than fifty dolls.

I love talking to other seniors. Some of them tell me they are lonely and I ask them if they like dolls. If they say "Yes," I give them dolls from my collection. One senior, Miss Freeman, would sit at the window waiting for me to come home from work every day. She loved to laugh. Sometimes she would say, "I was very lonely today." I did not want her to be lonely and the next day, I went to visit her with two little dolls in my bag.

"Miss Freeman, do you like dolls?" She told me how she used to have dolls when she was a little girl. I took the dolls out of the bag and she was beside herself with laughter. "Look at their faces!" She looked so happy and she sat them on her piano and that was the dolls' new home. She would still be at the window sometimes when I came home from work with a smile on her face. She told me that she talked to the dolls every morning and that she felt less lonely now.

Giving and sharing things always brings me real joy. When I share with others they seem to beam with joy. These are the happiest moments of my life.

49

I THOUGHT WE HAD EVERYTHING, BUT WE DIDN'T HAVE MUCH

Eileen Sawyer

G rowing up in the 1930s and 1940s has happy memories for me because my parents shielded me from worries such as the war or financial concerns. There were three important houses in my childhood—my family's house in Brighton, the local movie house, and my grandparents' house in Canada. Each provided me with a safe haven from any worries. We kids didn't have a care in the world. We had no responsibilities. My mother and father never raised their voices. My father couldn't swear, not even to say "damn." We had a very happy house. My mother never drove a car or had any desire to. I'll describe her as small, petite woman in a housedress with an apron over it. She was always happy and looked on the bright side of problems of the day. She loved her home and was always in it. A clean house was important to her, so she was always cleaning every day except Sunday. She was a great cook and made all her own bread, rolls, and biscuits. In the evenings, she would knit or crochet. I don't remember her ever just sitting idle. My father came from a very poor family. He was in awe of having my sister and me. He just loved everything we did. He wanted to make a better life for us than what he'd had.

We lived on Electric Avenue in Brighton, a short street with four houses. Our apartment was on the second floor of a three-family house. Mother, Dad, my sister Andrea (my only sibling), and I shared this five-room apartment. I shared a bedroom with my sister. The kitchen had a black stove heated by oil. Beside it was a small oil hot water tank. It gave little hot water, enough for washing dishes. We washed the dishes in a cast-iron sink on white legs under a window. A few feet from the sink was soapstone double sink, one side for washing clothes and the other side for rinsing them. My mother used a scrub board with a wooden frame and corrugated aluminum, and a bar of Fels-Naptha brown soap. Mother said it was the same as a washing machine. At the end of the kitchen was a back door leading to the back hall. We had a good-sized back porch, so Dad put up a swing for us. We would eat our lunch out there sometimes or take our dollhouse and its furniture outside and play for hours. When it came time for a bath, Mother heated water on the stove and carried it to the bathtub. On one side of the kitchen was a pantry for our dishes, pots and pans, and for storing food. In the big back hall, Mom kept the icebox with a block of ice to keep food cold. When she needed ice, which was often in the summer, she put a piece of cardboard that read "ice" in the living room window. The iceman came around every day on a horse-drawn wagon filled with blocks of ice. Seeing the sign in the window, he would stop, get his pick, and carry a block upstairs and put it in the icebox. He wore a rubber top to protect him from the cold ice. The other side of this piece of cardboard read "oil." When we needed oil, Mom turned the ice card over and put the other side in the window and the same procedure took place. We had a coal furnace in the cellar. We had a sign for the coalman, also. We called him "the coalman."

We ate in the kitchen; supper was our big meal when Dad came home from work. The dining room was used for company. The living room we all used. Unless it was bad weather, my sister Andrea and I were always outside. We had plenty of friends and we would jump rope, play hopscotch, hide-and-seek, jacks, tag, marbles, dolls, and go roller and ice skating, bike riding, and sledding.

There was a brick house near us for sale for five thousand dollars. My mother wanted to buy it, but my father worried about the cost with the Depression and all. My mother didn't want him to worry, so they chose not to buy it. In the 1960s when I went to buy my first house, my parents gave me the down payment. That's how much my happiness meant to my father. He didn't want a house for himself, but he wanted one for my sister and me.

Our entertainment was the radio. We loved to listen to Jack Benny, *The Shadow, Superman,* and *The Phantom.* Because it was wartime, we had to prepare for air raids. If we were in the house when the sirens sounded, shades had to be pulled down to put the house in darkness and the radio had to be turned off. If we were outside, we had to hide or run onto someone's porch. If in a car, we pulled to the side of the road and shut the lights off. When the sirens stopped, everything went back to normal. Also at this time, ration books were given to each household. Limits were put on milk, eggs, bread, bananas, soap, tea, cheese, sugar, and meat. You had to have a coupon for sugar or butter, and you still had to pay for it. Even with all of this going on, we were never afraid. I wasn't scared when the sirens went off. One time my mother started to say the rosary when she heard the sirens, but my father told her to stop, "You're scaring the kids." He did allow her to say the rosary during thunder and lighting storms.

Brighton Center had a movie house called the Egyptian, and I spent a lot of time there as a child. It was beautiful like the Boston Opera House. It was fancy outside, and the inside had gorgeous curtains, beautiful seats, and a beautiful stage. On the weekends we went to the movies. Saturday morning was for children with cartoons and a feature film. Families went in the afternoon or evenings. They ran continuous performances, and you could go whenever you liked and stay as long as you liked. For ten cents, you could see a main feature, a supporting feature, a cartoon, and a newsreel. They would change every week. The newsreels didn't faze me. The movies were pure fun. I loved the movie house. I lived in their world. I wanted to be a movie star. One of the games we played was movie star. One person would give hints about a star and the rest of us would have to guess who it was. The winner would then get a turn to pick the movie star.

Mom was born in Canada and came to the United Stated in the 1920s. She lived with her aunt in Andover and became a U.S. citizen not long after. We were often told how great our country was and that it offered so many opportunities. She came from a large family. Her mother was a teacher and her father a farmer. They also owned a store. Because they were so fortunate, they were able to help their neighbors. They all loved music and had so much talent. They played piano, keyboard, violin, harmonica, accordion, guitar, and ukulele, and sang and danced. It was always a party at my grandparents when I visited them during the summer.

I spent a lot of summer vacations in Canada. John and Veronica Peters (my mother's parents) had a big farm on hundreds of acres. Thinking back on those summers with my grandparents in Canada brings back so many memories. As I recall, there was no electricity or plumbing, yet each room had a kerosene lamp. The bathroom was outside and called an outhouse. They had a big red barn for the horses and cows. Chickens were in the hen house, sheep in the fields. Grandma was always knitting hats, mittens, sweaters, and blankets, and the yarn came from the sheep. Grandpa would cut the wool from the sheep and take it to the mill to have it spun into yarn. Her knitting kept them warm all winter. A large vegetable garden kept them in food all year. In the house they had a root cellar off the kitchen. A cover on the floor lifted up and a set of stairs led to a dirt room. I remember it as being cold and damp. It was filled with jars of vegetables, jellies, and fruit that she had preserved. The smell of Grandma's house was awesome. She was always baking bread and pies. Being a city girl, farm life was another world. They taught me to milk a cow, which I can't say I enjoyed but I did enjoy feeding the chickens and horses and riding in the horse-drawn wagon. This was their transportation. The cooking was done on the big stove. Meals came from the garden. Grandma made her own butter and ice cream. We would spend time outside picking blueberries and raspberries and then come in and have a bowl. She would pour cream on top — so delicious.

My parents didn't talk about the war or anything that might worry us children, even though my two uncles were in the war. One was MIA and the other was killed in France. My grandfather was killed in a wagon accident. This all happened in a few weeks. My parents never talked about any of this in front of us. My father would listen to the news on the radio so we heard some about the war. Money was never discussed in front of me or my sister. My mother never mentioned when she had a bill due. As an adult, I came to understand how much effort my parents put into protecting me from what was going on in the world. I feel so blessed to have lived and shared this wonderful life. I see now that we didn't have much, but as a child, I thought we had everything.

LIFE IN A TENEMENT

Marion Fennell Connolly

My grandchildren sometimes ask me what it was like to grow up poor in Boston. I don't know where to begin to describe what it was like living in a tenement in the 1940s to teenagers who can't imagine such a life.

Life in a cold-water flat was an experience in itself. Rent was seventeen dollars a month for five rooms, and my parents paid $4.25 weekly because they never seemed to be able to put the whole month's rent together. The landlord came to collect the rent. When my parents were late with the payment, I (being the oldest) delivered it, even though I was just eight or ten years old. I would walk to Dudley Station, take the streetcar up Dudley Street, get off at St. Patrick's Church, and walk across the street to the landlord's house.

The most delicious meal we had was mashed potatoes piled in the middle of the plate like an island with string beans stuck on it and a piece of meatloaf on top. My mother would pour gravy made from Campbell's tomato soup over it. Occasionally we would have spaghetti with tomato soup for a sauce. The soup was mixed with

water instead of milk, because milk was too expensive. I still love tomato soup.

The only method to heat water was to boil it on the black iron stove that we would polish periodically. This stove produced the only heat for the five rooms. A gallon glass oil container stood near the stove on some sort of a stand and was connected to the stove with a small, narrow pipe. We could buy a five-gallon can of oil from the oilman, but only when my parents had extra money. When we couldn't afford that, I would be sent to the local variety store with a gallon glass jug to buy some oil in the middle of winter. I remember how heavy that jug was when it was full, and I would have to set it down several times in the snow to rest.

My mother put a card in the front window if she wanted oil or ice that day. As I remember, the oil and ice were delivered by the same truck. Usually we bought a twenty-five-cent piece of ice that the iceman would chop off with an ice pick. We had a rectangular, black soapstone sink that was about three and a half feet long and seven inches deep. It had only one faucet. We would fill a basin with the boiled water to wash dishes, and we used the same method to wash ourselves. Dirty clothes would be sent to the wet wash, which would be picked up by a truck and returned wet. The clothes would be hung on a line from the kitchen window to the electrical pole to dry.

The horse and wagon would come around on certain days with vegetables and fruit, and also the ragman came around with his horse and wagon shouting, "Any ol' rags?" Nate's Meat Market was on one corner of our block, the First National store was on another corner, and Al's and Sammy's variety stores were on the other corners.

At Christmastime in 1940, money was especially scarce. My mother wrote a letter to Post Santa, which was a charity program run by the *Boston Post,* which was then one of the largest newspapers in the country. Her request had to be verified by a nun at our school, who confirmed that my parents had no money for toys for us. On Christmas Eve, there was a knock on the door and when we opened it, a man delivered a box that contained a toy for each child. How excited I was! Although I don't remember my toy, I do remember the little train given to my brother. It was a small tin circular plate that a single train ran around on. I don't remember how it operated but it must have been a windup toy.

When I was between the ages of eight and twelve, we played jump rope every summer morning. There were a lot of little girls in the tenements and we always had plenty of playmates. We would play in the middle of St. Francis de Sales Street, a side street next to our grammar school. We also played games called jack stones, jack knife, and aggies. I loved aggies and at one of our games my friend Patsy and her friend Issy scrambled the pot and ran. During our grammar school years, we would sometimes smoke cigarettes. During the war years and in the section of Roxbury known as "Leaky Roof" you could buy looseys (single cigarettes) for a penny apiece.

I would go to Al's corner store with a note one of my friends would have written backhand to "give Marion 5 looseys" and sign my mother's name, and for five pennies I had five cigarettes. Then five of us would go to someone's cellar to smoke and leave our coats outside so they would not smell of smoke. I was never caught but one of my friends was. Ironically, I stopped smoking at age twenty.

The three-decker tenements would get hot in summer, and people would sit out on their front stairs. One night, my friends and I decided to walk to Simmons Street where there were a few factories. It was just a block from my house. We went there to smoke one of our looseys on the loading dock of the mattress factory. We started home at about nine o'clock. About an hour later, after I had gone to bed, a huge explosion occurred. Everyone in the entire neighborhood came running out of their houses. The street was jammed with people; children were out in the street in their nightclothes. The sky was all lit up. I was very frightened. This was during World War II, and I thought we were being bombed. I always thought the Simmons mattress factory had blown up, but recently I asked librarians at the Boston Public Library to do some research, and they told me that the explosion had occurred at the varnish plant of the National Chair Company at 80 Hampshire Street; it was June 12, 1944.

We didn't have a bathtub, but we did bathe. We lived a block from the Cabot Street Bathhouse. It was open six days a week with Mondays and Thursdays reserved for women and girls. It had a swimming pool and for a nickel we got a grey cotton bathing suit, a small bar of soap, and two dishtowel-sized towels. It was hard to come by the nickel. I remember having a penny and guarding it, hoping to get some other pennies together to go to the bathhouse. On the second floor was a gymnasium, lockers, and showers. This part was all free. The shower stalls were all private with marble partitions, a small, attached bench, and a wooden door that had a latch-type lock. When we were teenagers and old enough to go to the showers in the evening by ourselves, even my friends who had bathtubs at home preferred to go to the bathhouse. It became a social time for us as we set our hair in pin curls and then walked home. There was also basketball to play in the gym where the girls could only run on one half of the court. The forwards for one team would be on one half of the court and their guards on the other half to block the forwards of the opposing team from making a basket. It was great fun.

In the cold winter months, my parents would pull their mattress to the kitchen floor and shut off three of the five rooms. I would sleep with my younger brothers, and my youngest sister would sleep between my parents. In the morning the mattress would be put back in their room only to be dragged out the next very cold night. As I got older, I would sleep in the small front bedroom with my sister, Mary, who was nine years younger. The room had a kerosene heater that used the same oil as the kitchen stove. The bedroom was so cold that I could see my own breath. I would leave my clothes on a chair beside my bed. I would take each piece of clothing under the blanket to get dressed before I got out of bed. Many a morning my face would have black soot near my nose from the circulating heater. I can't imagine how much soot I breathed in during those nights. Many, many years later this type of heater was prohibited because they were so dangerous.

As a young teenager, about fourteen or fifteen years of age, I had my first paid babysitting job, at which I earned fifty cents for the entire night. There were not many jobs because most parents couldn't afford a sitter. I sat for a young couple that had two very young children. They lived in the Eustis Street Housing Project in Roxbury. My family didn't have a telephone, so they contacted me when they visited neighbors who lived across from me. When they came home

62

WEST ROXBURY

around one in the morning I would have about a fifteen-minute walk home alone at that hour through Dudley Station and along Roxbury Street. I remember feeling a little frightened. They had a telephone, so when I sat I would call a few of my girlfriends to come over, and we would call up boys on the phone and giggle and laugh but never leave our names. There was a smoked shoulder left in the refrigerator one night, and my friends and I ate the whole ham. My friends left before they came home. I was never asked to sit again.

My old neighborhood no longer exists. Back then it was known as St. Francis de Sales parish, and if anyone in Boston wanted to know where in Roxbury you lived, they wouldn't say, "What street?" They would say, "What parish?" But for those of us who lived in the parish, we called our neighborhood "Leaky Roof." Downing Street was located behind the Cabot Street Bathhouse, and the houses on that street had leaky roofs so the area became known as such.

These days Madison Park Technical Vocational High School has replaced all the variety stores, taverns, churches, schools, the bathhouse, factories, and tenements in St. Francis de Sales parish. I still have my many friends from childhood in Leaky Roof, and I could pick up the phone and talk to them as though it were yesterday — about the dances at Hibernian Hall on Saturday night, Sunday night dances at St. Alphonsus Hall, and the young men we met from Cherry Valley, Roxbury, whom four of us married.

KEEP CALM AND CARRY ON

Eileen Bradley

"Who remembers July of 1955?" Dorothy Dorsey asked as we began our memoir class. My mind immediately returned to that tumultuous summer when Boston was inundated with victims of the polio epidemic. Many children were affected. The symptoms were a cold with headache and chills, with a chance of paralysis setting in. It caused inflammation of the spinal cord, and the disease was called "poliomyelitis" or "infantile paralysis."

In 1955, my husband Peter, our six-year-old nephew Kevin, our three-year-old son Michael, and our five-month-old daughter Elizabeth, and I had just moved from an attic apartment in Dorchester to a second-floor apartment in the two-family house we had just purchased in West Roxbury. The neighborhood was similar to the one I had grown up in (Roxbury) with the church, school, library, and supermarket all within walking distance. Ours was a short street teeming with children, and Kevin soon joined them playing outside. He contracted polio with no ill effects, but Elizabeth sustained a debilitating paralysis mainly in her legs (she continues to use crutches to this day). Her following years consisted of hospitalizations, surgeries, and physical therapy, and then learning to walk with braces and crutches. Many family decisions were based on what was best for Elizabeth because of polio, including where the girls went to school. They had all been accepted at Girls' Latin School, but I didn't want Elizabeth traveling to Dorchester, so they all attended Ursuline Academy in Dedham.

In July 1958, a moving van appeared in our neighborhood. As I watched the wicker chairs being unloaded, I thought someone interesting was moving in next door. Later, I met that young mother of three boys, Joan McManus. At that time, we each had newborns—she had Brian and I had Diana—and our husbands worked the night shift. That created the nucleus of our friendship. Over the next forty years, I would discover every day how much we had in common.

Joan was slender and stylish with blue eyes and always had the latest hairdo. She was fastidious in her appearance. An excellent housekeeper, she also sewed beautifully. We were the "Thelma and Louise" of our era. She had the driver's license, and we made time to spend together outside of our homes. We laughed and cried our way through fun and tragedy almost on a daily basis.

The closest connection between us was our concern for our children. Her three boys had hemophilia and my Elizabeth had polio. We exchanged babysitting services for the children's various hospital visits and supported each other during the ups and downs of those visits. We were constant companions on shopping expeditions, sewing projects, and daily cups of tea. We spent many vacations together

when her family joined us on Cape Cod. Our children grew up together, partied together, and attended each other's proms. Even our
husbands enjoyed each other's company and played golf together.

Joan went to work at Catholic Memorial High School and suggested that I apply for a job teaching there. I did and we spent seventeen years working together. Joan and I chaperoned the Catholic
Memorial prom with our husbands. It was a memorable event since
I had graduated from high school during World War II, and my
small school didn't have a prom. Joan and I had some differences:
she was an only child and I was one of seven. Yet, our families
joined forces and our friendship was a unique forty-year compan-
ionship without rancor. It lasted until she died in 1996. Not a day
goes by when I don't think, "What would Joan say?"

Because of her polio, I enrolled Elizabeth in a ballet class at Boston
Ballet for exercise and took my younger daughter Diana along.
Diana loved it and that chance arrangement became her passion.
She attended the Boston Conservatory and spent her college years
singing and dancing in the musical theater program. Her college
summers were spent at the Orleans Inn on Cape Cod as part of the
entertainment and because we had a summer home on the Cape, our
evenings were spent at the inn. Several of her classmates, whom we
dubbed "the Show Mates," lived with us during the summer. As so
aptly described in their repertoire, "the joint was jumping." We had
cousins by the dozens and my Uncle Jim, a dapper Irish gentleman
with a shock of white hair and thick brogue, had been a Gilbert &
Sullivan performer and he provided the best entertainment in years,
singing, dancing, and advising Diana's classmates.

How we acquired our vacation home is an interesting story. In 1960, I attended an auction of the McCloud Bakery on Centre Street and while there, I struck up a conversation about vacation opportunities with a distinguished elderly gentleman called Captain Michael. Having told him that we had just returned from a rainy week in Yarmouth in a small rented cottage on a crowded street, he suggested Nauset Beach on the lower Cape as an alternative to the busy Yarmouth area. I followed his advice and planned a trip to a part of the Cape that was new to us.

Captain Michael had several lots of land for sale and the next thing I knew I was the proud owner of a half-acre of buildable land in Eastham where we have vacationed every summer since that chance meeting on Centre Street. It was one of the best decisions I have ever made and it led an unbelievable experience that has enhanced our family life beyond expectations, but we never built on the land. We looked for a builder in 1963 and then a local realtor, Louis Gregory, suggested we look at a cottage that he had for sale that had just been reduced in price. Lo and behold, this summer home in Eastham had been rented by my cousin the previous year. It was a year-round home on a half-acre lot, walking distance to the bay beach, with six bedrooms, one and a half bathrooms, a dining room, and a living room with a large fireplace. It was perfect for us. We bought it immediately and have enjoyed it for the past forty-nine years. Originally we called it "Castle Rag" but now it is "The Enchanted Cottage" with a sign over the front door that says *Cead Mile Failte*, which is Gaelic for "a hundred thousand welcomes." The Irish have a zest for life as demonstrated in their daily attitude and their questions are, "What's for dinner?" and "Where's the dance?"

My husband and I still live in the home we bought fifty-seven years ago in West Roxbury. Our children are adults now and I am accused of not telling them I love them. My excuse is that I'm Irish and not demonstrative. They are all college graduates with various degrees and careers in education. Elizabeth grew up right along with them. She married, has two adult children, a full-time job, and she drives through Boston like a cabbie. Elizabeth works with the elderly in the state government; Michael teaches in Dedham; Diana teaches musical theatre, social etiquette, and ballroom dancing; Christopher is employed at Framingham State; and Jennifer teaches in Norwood. I love them and I am proud of their accomplishments, especially in the field of education. Who knew the outcome would be so positive?

Helping

THE JOHNSON NURSING HOME

Jack Casey

In 1958, my wife Rita and I moved from Maine to West Roxbury with our four children who ranged in age from five months to eighteen years old. We both had to work to support our family. That's when the Johnson Nursing Home became a part of our lives. My wife was five foot two, slim with black, curly hair, and always cheerful. She was a registered nurse and wore a white uniform with white shoes that she polished every night. She was very organized. Our kids and our house were always spotless. She applied for a job at the Johnson Nursing Home, located at 42 Wren Street, less than five minutes from our house. It was nestled in the middle of a residential neighborhood made up mostly of single-family homes. The nursing home sat next to the elementary school our children attended. It served thirty-two female patients who needed various levels of care. The Johnson Nursing Home was unique in that it didn't feel institutional. If you drove by, you wouldn't know it was a nursing home. It didn't even have a sign out front. It was nothing like what people think of nursing homes today, not like the Deutsches Altenheim in Boston (German Centre for Extended Care). Typically, nursing homes back then were not somewhere you would want to be. But the Johnson Nursing Home was clean and neat, somewhere families would want to visit their loved ones because the patients were given such good care and the facility was welcoming.

The owner, Tony, was often onsite, yet he knew nothing about how to run the place. For him it was an investment. He was a really good man and a generous person. As a family, we always remember the time he bought a new bright blue Cadillac, and as he walked into the home, he tossed the keys to my seventeen-year-old daughter and said, "Drive your mother home."

In a very short time, Rita was in charge of the nursing home. She hired our children and their teenage friends to work there. Our three sons always shoveled the long driveway and three fire escapes. At one time or another, our three daughters worked in the home doing various jobs: helping in the kitchen, delivering food, visiting the patients and singing for them. As teenagers, they would always be dancing around to popular music. One day a girl fell through the window and from that day on was known as "Crash." My wife was blessed to have two young nurse's aides who did an outstanding job tending to the patients. The nurse's aides didn't wear uniforms; they were just eighteen-year-old kids, but very helpful.

While working at the Johnson Nursing Home, my wife had three more children and would often bring our youngest, also named Rita, to work with her. My wife set up a crib on the third floor where baby Rita would nap. As she grew older, Rita would visit the patients who loved to see her and talk to her. Like all nursing homes, Johnson was subject to state inspections. Obviously, those would have been hindered by having a young child running around. When the inspectors came, sometimes unannounced, the nurse's aides would run Rita up the back stairs to the third floor until the inspector left.

The kitchen was located in the basement of the three-story, Victorian-style home. My wife's sister was the cook and did a fabulous job considering the limited space and facilities she had to work with. In order to deliver the meals to patients, an old-fashioned dumbwaiter was used to lift meals to the first and second floors. Just off the kitchen was a small nook with a table and two benches for breaks and enjoying refreshing cups of tea. Many times my wife would sit there with a favorite patient who had enough mobility to navigate the stairs. The laundry room was also in the basement and there they washed all the linens and laundry. They used the pipes running across the ceiling to hang sheets to dry. My wife sometimes would pop out from behind the hanging sheets and surprise our youngest daughter.

The nursing home had its own activities director, who rode a large motorcycle and did some entertaining with her guitar playing. A favorite activity of the patients was bowling, and my mother, who entered the home when she was about eighty, was their champion bowler. While a resident there, my mother had a partial amputation of one of her legs and received great care and attention from the entire staff. I was greatly impressed and learned a real lesson watching my mother stoically accept this adjustment.

Running along the front of the house was a long porch where the patients could sit and enjoy the nice weather during the summertime.

Rita Casey in her nursing uniform

One day, my wife was checking a patient on the porch, and the lady asked Rita if she could see the monkey swinging on a tree across the street. My wife kindly ignored the remark because the lady was often a little confused. Two weeks later, the patient mentioned it again and pointed to the tree. Sure enough, there was a small monkey in the tree that the lady in the house kept as a pet. From that time on, my daughter used to go out there and watch the monkey.

When Rita retired, the crowd we hung around with threw her a surprise retirement party at a neighbor's house. These neighbors were always joking with her and giving her the business from their porches whenever she walked past on her way to work. When she got the invitation to their party, she decided she was going to fix them. Rita didn't know it was a retirement party for her. She thought she would play a gag on them and went dressed as a bag lady. She climbed through a hole in the fence surrounding the neighbor's yard. When he opened the door, she entered by kind of crawling in on her knees only to be greeted by a room full of people dressed for a party in her honor. Rita didn't go home to change her clothes. She stayed dressed as a bag lady for her own retirement party.

After Rita retired, she became a member of a church group whose members sewed bandages and johnnies to be shipped to the mission hospitals in Africa. True to form, because of her organizational skills, she was soon running the group. They met every Wednesday morning and would deliver the product once a month to St. Elizabeth Hospital, which shipped them overseas.

I still meet people whose mothers were confined to Johnson Nursing Home, and they express their gratitude for the great care Rita and her staff provided. Rita was a rather tiny lady but a bundle of energy, always ready and willing to assist those in need.

FOLLOWING IN PAPA'S FOOTSTEPS

Betsaida Gutiérrez

I was born in Coamo Arriba, Puerto Rico. When I was three, my brother and I went to live with my paternal grandparents. Because my father worked in San Juan, he only came to visit us on the weekends. My grandfather raised me as his daughter, and I called him Papá.

My grandfather, Juan Evangelisto Rodriguez, was born in Puerto Rico in 1897. He was a white man, a descendent of the Spaniards. He had white hair and crystal blue eyes. He was a quiet man who went to work for the landowners at an early age to support his brothers and sisters. He worked on the sugar cane plantations seven days a week; he could only rest four hours during the week and three hours on weekends. I imagine he got paid pennies. At age eight, one my chores was to bring him his lunch in the field. I would say to him, "Can I help you, Papá?" He always replied in a soft voice, "No, you have wobbly legs and you could fall."

Later in life, Papá went from working for the landowners to becoming his own boss. He rented land from people he knew and trusted. The land was fertile for planting rice, tobacco, squash, root vegetables, pigeon peas, beans, and corn. I remember him getting up at six o'clock in the morning, drinking his black coffee, and going off to work.

Papá was well known in our town and people addressed him as Don Lito. To call someone "don" is the highest form of respect. He attended all the funerals for people in Barrio Coamo Arriba and surrounding towns. He was well known by the mayor of Coamo. My grandfather advocated for and got the residents indoor plumbing and water delivery through pipes from the *represa* (reservoir). The mayor of Coamo held a celebration to inaugurate the *represa* and presented my grandfather an award for his work. Papá passed away at age 102.

I finished high school in Puerto Rico and I wanted to continue my education, but my grandparents wouldn't let me. In those days, it wasn't considered important for a woman to get a higher education. My aunt wanted me to become a nurse, but I didn't want to because I am afraid of needles. When I was nineteen, my grandfather sent me to live in the U.S. so that I could have a better life and find a husband who could take care of me. He didn't want me to have the hard life that he had working on a farm.

I came to live with my aunt in Mission Hill. I felt like a prisoner because I stayed all day alone in the house. I only went out to go to church. My chore was to soak and boil the beans for supper. I didn't speak English; I didn't have job. I said to myself, "I need to learn this language."

Eventually, a Latino man helped me find a job. He took me to fill out an application for a job in a curtain factory in Chinatown. He also taught me how to get back and forth to work. When I went to work, I got lost. I couldn't speak English so asked people directions, but they were mostly Chinese who responded to me in sign language that they didn't speak English, either.

I wore high-heel shoes and a miniskirt to work even though it was winter. My legs were frozen, and finally my aunt got me a coat, which I wore in winter and in summer. I didn't realize that wearing high heels and a miniskirt downtown made me look like a woman of ill repute. I made friends in the factory who showed me the stores where I bought more clothes and fancy jewelry. I went to school to learn English and to learn a skill. I worked at an insurance company proofreading their figures for three years.

In 1975, I met my husband and we had a daughter. I volunteered with City Life/La Vida Urbana. During this time, I participated in the Wake Up the Earth Festival, which made me realize I wanted to become more active outside my home. My friend Pat Feeley invited me to work on a newspaper. I got very involved with the people in my community. I organized street clean-ups. Then I worked with the Jamaica Plain Neighborhood Development Corporation. I got volunteers to translate the written plans informing the community about the opening of the Orange Line, and we formed the Latino Caucus. I worked at the JPNDC for seven years. I also worked as an advocate at City Life/La Vida Urbana to empower Latinos and other minorities. During this time I completed my undergraduate education at Cambridge College. In one class, we read a poem about a grandfather and I began to cry. I realized how much my grandfather meant to me and how great he was.

I became a case manager for ABCD (Action for Boston Community Development), then went to work for Friendship Works and became the Jamaica Plain volunteer coordinator of people assisting seniors. I also developed a program called the Circle of Friendship.

In 2010, a housing cooperative was named after to me in appreciation for my work. It is called the Doña Betsaida Gutiérrez Cooperative House at 363–365 Centre Street in Jamaica Plain. I wanted it to be called "Doña Betsaida" in memory of the respect I felt for Don Lito, *mi papá*.

I believe I have followed in my papá's footsteps. I have worked hard, respected my elders, and other people. I have advocated in many projects for affordable housing. I have received many awards for doing this work. I feel that I am the clone of my grandfather. I can't tell him how much I love him and how proud I am of him, or thank him for being a great papá. It is my dream come true to be able to write this memoir as a tribute to this great man.

BUBBLES THE CLOWN

Janice Beals Kelly

I started my volunteer clowning career at the age of forty-six. I guess I was a late bloomer. As a kid, I never saw clowns except at the circus. I don't know why I bought my first clown costume, but it changed my life. I liked clowning because I like kids. I wanted to have my own kids, but it didn't work out. I have clowned for sick children and their families, for special needs children, older adults, and with my nieces.

Every summer for nine years, I spent a week of my vacation clowning at Camp Sunshine on Sebago Lake in Maine, one of the first camps for children with cancer (we weren't allowed to say "terminally ill"). About ten of us from the Boston Gas Company went every summer. We had a trailer and slept two in a trailer. I went with my clown buddy, Bangles and Bones, from my clown alley, for five summers. Camp Sunshine was just starting out then; they needed at least a hundred or more volunteers to do everything from cooking to cleaning up and taking care of the children, from toddlers up to teenagers. The whole family came — the mothers, the fathers, the sick children, and their siblings.

The families and volunteers came up Sunday morning and left Friday afternoon. The parents and children had separate activities. The parents could take classes for coping with children with cancer or they could enjoy alone time while we took care of the children. The parents would also have a special dinner one night. I had the three- to five-year-olds. I was good with that age group because I spent a lot of time with my nieces who were also that age. I was a regular volunteer most of the time, but in the morning and afternoon I would put on my clown costume, put on a half-hour show, and have two new kids join me on stage. I had two kid-sized clown costumes for them to put on so they could join in and have their pictures taken. I put on music and we danced, stuff that kids liked. At the end of the week we had a little show with all the kids including the teenagers. My group always did *Twinkle Twinkle Little Star.*

Once I had one little five-year-old boy who was difficult with everyone else. He didn't understand that he was so rough. I told him, "Everyone else has thrown you out of their group. Shape up and you can stay with me." He called me "Mrs. Mulligan," after the tough teacher from the musical *Annie*. When he was asked to join another group, he responded, "I'm going to stick with Mrs. Mulligan. She's the only one who would give me a chance." My summers at Camp Sunshine inspired me to start clowning for kids year-round.

My cousin Ellen's husband Richie belonged to the Sons of Italy, and he asked me to dress up like a clown to entertain the special needs children his group was performing for. He said they would love it. I was getting dressed at Ellen's house when she asked me my clown name. She suggested "Bubbles" because she said I had a bubbly personality (you know how relatives think you're swell). I thought it was a good luck name so I used it for my clown name. I worked with a man at Boston Gas Company named Joe, who was called "The Family Man." He called me Bubbles and he called my friend Sunny, who also worked with us, "Tiny Bubbles." She was four foot eleven, and I was five foot six.

The minute kids saw me dressed up in my costume they wanted to dance with me. I was thrilled. I figured I was a big hit. All of a sudden I saw three beautiful clowns come through the door. Next to them, I looked like a sad sack. The kids yelled, "Bubbles, your friends are here." I thought I was in big trouble and figured they belonged to a clown union. They came over to me and asked, "What alley do you belong to?" I said, "I've been in many alleys, but never belonged to one." They laughed out loud and told me a clown club was called an "alley." They belonged to the South Shore Joeys, Alley 159A. I was invited to come to their monthly meetings in Weymouth. They taught me how to put on makeup. I also learned that clowns have strict rules of conduct. A clown can never drink alcohol or any other beverage or eat in public, especially in front of the kids.

There are four types of clowns — white face, hobo, Auguste, and pirouette clowns. I became a white face clown. My face and neck was all white. I had a red rubber nose that was glued on, a little glitter on my face, but the trick was putting my mouth on. I would exaggerate my red painted lips with a curve at the end of my mouth to mimic a smile. I also wore a wig, a hat, gloves, and shoes to match the custom. I usually wore sneakers because clown shoes cost about a hundred dollars, and I would only use them occasionally in competition. One time I won second prize in the white face competition.

The South Shore Joeys held clown conventions at a hotel in Plymouth. They would give you lunch and dinner—a big dinner with entertainment—then a brunch on Sunday morning. Each convention had a theme. One had a doctor theme, another was Irish night, and another had a flapper night. They were great family events. I took my nieces, Courtney and Shannon, five times. I had costumes made for them. My nieces spent every other weekend with me. They were the loves of my life. I didn't have any children of my own, but they were like my own. On Saturdays we attended different workshops: balloons, makeup, juggling, how to create your clown personality, and many other skills. Arrow, a hobo clown, taught me how to blow up animal balloons. He could make all kinds of fancy balloon animals. I explained to the kids that I was a new clown and suggested we play "Adopt a Puppy Day" because I only knew how to make balloon dogs at the time. They could pick the color balloon they wanted and I would turn it into a balloon dog. They all yelled, "Yea!" Later Arrow told me I was the hit of the day.

Our alley received a lot of requests to perform at Christmastime, and one year we went to a party for children with special needs. This time I brought a baby doll with me. I called it "Baby." A little girl about ten years old asked if this was the Baby Jesus that people were always talking about. I said, "No, honey, the Baby Jesus is in church." That made sense to her. The special needs boys always wanted to dance with me and sometimes they wanted me to sit in their lap. I told them my clown husband said I could dance

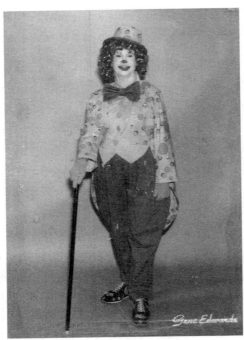

Janice as Bubbles the Clown

with them, but no sitting on their laps because they were too good looking. The boys liked that and started to laugh and I danced off with them.

We also visited nursing homes. The first time I went I was the only clown who showed up. I went to the recreation room and there were many elderly people there. They had a piano player. I knew the words to a lot of old songs and asked them to help me with the songs, but no one volunteered. I went up to one of the elderly ladies and asked her to help me sing a song. She said, "Okay, you're pretty." As we started singing everybody joined in and then we started to dance. The other women complimented her on her singing. Two women put their arms around her, singing and dancing. It brought her out of her shell. As I was getting ready to leave, a nursing home employee informed me that the lady who sang with me had been there for about a month and had not mixed well before then. I took that as a compliment.

From 1986 to 1999, Boston Gas let us dress up as clowns and deliver Christmas gifts to needy children during work hours, and the company provided the gifts. One year, Boston Gas sent us to a day care center on Dudley Street in Roxbury to volunteer as part of a Christmas celebration. The children ranged in age from three to five years old. Joe was six foot two and dressed up as Santa while Barbara dressed up as a Barbie doll with a white-faced clown. Barbara also belonged to my clown alley. When the kids saw us, they screamed in fear and huddled in corners and under desks. We must have looked frightening to these very young black children, as we were very big white people with exaggerated made-up faces. We couldn't bribe them to come out with toys, our props, or to sit on Santa's lap. We left the toys around the Christmas tree and when the teacher announced we were leaving, we waved goodbye and then all the children eagerly waved goodbye to us.

I stopped clowning when my clown alley moved from Weymouth to Abington, too far for me to drive at night. As you get older, getting made up as a clown becomes a chore. Now I pick up my fellow seniors who don't drive for activities. We have a lot of classes at our Senior Center, Ethos. When I retired, my cousin was sick with cancer and I was with her for a year. I watched her two boys for two days a week. Those boys go to Boston Latin and they still like me. They're still with me to this day.

"The Clown's Prayer" is a poem or prayer that comedians of various sorts use for inspiration. The original author is unknown.

As I stumble through this life,
help me to create more laughter than tears,
dispense more cheer than gloom,
spread more cheer than despair.

Never let me become so indifferent,
that I will fail to see the wonders in the eyes of a child,
or the twinkle in the eyes of the aged.

Never let me forget that my total effort is to cheer people,
make them happy, and forget momentarily,
all the unpleasantness in their lives.

And in my final moment,
may I hear You whisper:
"When you made My people smile,
you made Me smile."

THE TOUGHEST JOB
I EVER LOVED

Robert Godino

Pres
dent Kennedy is credited with creating the Peace Corps in 1962, but it was Hubert Humphrey who introduced the bill in 1957. As a law student, I was interested in this idea of developing better relationships between countries by people helping people. After about six months of watching the program grow, and with a growing admiration of President Kennedy's administration, I volunteered to go to South America.

When I signed up, I was twenty-seven and one of the older volunteers. I had already graduated from college, spent three years in the navy, and attended law school. I joined twenty other men at the University of Washington—Seattle for training. We built a small garage from concrete blocks as practice for building rural schools. We were taught Spanish, and those of us considered proficient were sent to Puerto Rico for additional language classes and physical training. In spite of my age, I excelled in all of the physical activities. We ran two miles every morning down the entry road to Camp Crozier, out to the main road, and back to the dormitories and showers. I was

determined to be the first to finish every day. My Spanish language skills, however, were not as good. Still, I passed each test and was selected for assignment to the Dominican Republic.

In Santo Domingo, I met with the director who made the local site assignments. My first assignment was to assist a volunteer in Bani who was building a school out of adobe (mud and straw). The Bani school site was already well along, so my help wasn't needed. Next I was sent to a site in Las Matas de Farfan to help two volunteers start a school. I drew up plans for the building and found a site on a hill with a good view. We dug the foundation and then learned we had to wait for supplies and materials to arrive from CARE, a humanitarian organization.

During the delay I was sent to Mao, part of the Valverde region, to meet two other volunteers and build a school in Pueblo Nuevo. I met Luis Midence from New Jersey and Bill Glennon from Illinois, and moved into the house they shared in Mao. It had only two bedrooms and since I was the last to move in, I made a bedroom out of a small alcove. My bed was a cot, the portable fold-up kind typically used for camping, and I had a small set of drawers to store my clothes. A local woman named Felina worked as our housekeeper and shopped for us daily at the local market. She cooked regular Dominican food: salads, and rice and beans with chicken or goat meat. Our house did not have indoor plumbing, so she prepared our meals from an attached room in the rear of the house where there was a single faucet for cold water. Next to this room was our shower area and behind that an outhouse. Most of the other houses in Mao had modern kitchens and toilets, but we could not afford to rent them.

*Robert laying bricks at a school site in the
Dominican Republic*

Felina washed clothes in the backyard and used clotheslines for drying. I read a Peace Corps manual about some volunteers who had made a clothes washer, so I made one with a fifty-gallon barrel cut in half. A handle moved the piston in each barrel up and down. It worked pretty well. We could heat the water with a small charcoal fire under each barrel and drain it with spigots in the bottom. We wrung out the clothes by hand. An added benefit was that it was a good tub for Felina's young son, Edward.

Pueblo Nuevo was a small town about five miles from Mao that had a lot of kids and an old and decayed school. Most of the kids had the chore of carrying water to their homes from the river three miles away. They helped their mothers take clothes to the river for

94

washing and then used the family donkey to haul water back to the house for cooking. Luis and Bill had been working with the local officials and found that a school was needed. They held a meeting with the residents to find out if they had any special interests. What resi-

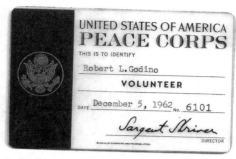

Robert's 1962 Peace Corps ID with Sargent Shriver's signature

dents said they needed, more than a school, was local water. Luis and Bill brought a group of well drillers to the town; they drilled a well and the whole town helped build a washroom and fountain at the site. Once everyone began using the local washroom, the kids were no longer busy hauling water and became bothersome during the day. The residents then decided that school would be a good way to keep kids busy. We asked local men if they would help us build the school if we supplied the materials. They agreed and we searched for a site. The plans were for a building twenty-five feet by fifty feet with a classroom and storage room. A farmer donated land, and we had started to dig a foundation near a tree in the field when it started to rain. When the rain stopped, we went back to the area and found the site underneath two feet of water. It was a long field and we discovered that it sloped six feet from one end to the other, so we changed our plans and dug the foundation at the high end.

We didn't have a telephone, but communicated with the director or the Peace Corps office via telegram. Though current Peace Corps

95

volunteers have cell phones and computers, they do not have vehicles. We had a robin's egg blue Jeep for getting around. When we drove into town each day, the local workers would gather. The kids would run to be the first to arrive so that they could bring the wheelbarrow full of tools to the building site. Once the materials from CARE were finally available for distribution, we were unfortunately delayed again because the cement mixer was damaged during delivery. While we waited for the parts, we made blocks. CARE provided us with a machine to make blocks for building; it compressed a mixture of soil, sand, and cement into a brick. The method took a lot of coordination: locating the proper soil, transporting it to the building site, mixing it, pressing the blocks, and curing the blocks for nearly thirty days before we could use them. Everyone liked to see how many we could make while acting as the "brick master."

Once in a while, employees of United Fruit Company would invite us to their beach house in the northern part of the country, a place called Punta Russia. We had a great time snorkeling and swimming. During one of these trips I set out to mark out some vacant land that I thought was an ideal location for a beach house. I found out during my fortieth reunion that Luis, who married a local woman, had claimed the land as a homestead and built a summer house there.

When we finally got the mixer working, we poured the foundation and mixed mortar for block walls for the Puerto Nuevo school. During this phase of construction, we learned that President Kennedy had been assassinated in Dallas. All the people in Pueblo Nuevo were crying and offering us their sympathy. They loved Kennedy as much as one of their own heroes. Originally the town

Building the John F. Kennedy Rural School with local help

had planned for the school to be named for one of the Dominican national heroes, but the villagers decided right then to name it after John F. Kennedy.

We worked with different men each day. Some men paid others to work for them during the harvest or on holidays. The Dominicans celebrated one or two holidays every month, and we would of course celebrate with them. On March 17, we started work as usual, but around noon I remembered that it was Saint Patrick's Day. I announced that in Boston it was a holiday and we always had a big parade, and the Dominicans enthusiastically yelled, *"Viva San Patricio!"* We all took the rest of the day off and had our own party in a local bar. When we got back to Mao, a group of helicopter pilots were having a party and singing Irish songs. We were quick to join in.

Most days we stayed in town after work and met residents who wanted to learn English. The Peace Corps central office sent us books for classes, and we taught conversational English for an hour every evening. My class of four young women and one young man could say "Paark the caar" as good as any Bostonian.

During the last month of my Peace Corps term, I helped the Mao residents start a Boy Scout troop. I became the local scoutmaster until we could find someone to take over. The assistant manager of the local bank had three boys who wanted to join, so he was happy to become scoutmaster. One of their projects was to raise plants in a garden and sell the produce at the local market. They used the money to buy Scout uniforms and neckerchiefs.

The John F. Kennedy Rural School was dedicated in October 1964. During my visit to the Dominican Republic for the fiftieth Peace Corps reunion in March 2012, I met a current volunteer, Emma Swift, who is also from Boston and works in Mao. She visited Pueblo Nuevo and emailed me photographs of the town as it is now. The town has a new, two-story school that replaced the old school, but I was pleased to learn that the school we built was used for more than thirty years and they continue to call it John F. Kennedy Rural School. I will always remember my Peace Corps experience as the toughest job I ever loved.

TEACHING AT THE BURKE

Sherrard Mowry Hamilton

In 1972, I moved to Boston from the Midwest and worked as a substitute English teacher in various Boston public schools while applying for permanent teaching positions. One day, while substitute teaching a high school class at the all-white "D Street Annex" in South Boston, I nearly put on my coat and walked out of the school. No matter what subject we were covering—grammar, writing, or short stories—the students would burst out with racist, anti-Black remarks. I was disturbed. I was scared. Later, I demanded that the Court Street office deploying substitutes never again assign me to South Boston.

In contrast, I felt instantly at home while substitute teaching at the Jeremiah E. Burke High School in Dorchester. The all-female, all African American, student population at "the Burke" was receptive to learning and appreciative of my teaching. Many students were from the Caribbean islands, and many more lived in the Columbia Point Housing Project in South Boston. I knew I could love these kids and do a good job there.

Once I passed the Boston teachers' exam and had my job interview, I requested assignment to the Burke and began the next phase of my teaching career. Miss Spencer, a fellow teacher and lifelong Boston resident, took me under her wing and introduced me to Boston history, politics, and sports teams. My colleagues and I were entertained by Miss Spencer's Irish gift of gab, her astonishing memory, and great sense of humor. She often teased me about being a "Midwestern farm girl." Having grown up in Evanston, Illinois, a sophisticated suburb of Chicago, I'd never lived on or near a farm, but her jokes were a way of including me and welcoming me to the Burke community.

My favorite class was a group of super-smart seniors to whom I taught *The Scarlet Letter* by Nathaniel Hawthorne. How we loved talking about Hester, Pearl, and Dimmesdale; together, we made those characters come alive. These fine young women and I enjoyed a mutual admiration society. However, that was my last year teaching in an all-female school; soon afterward, the school became co-educational. Teaching became more difficult because the boys were not as receptive to learning and could be disruptive. Still I loved being at the Burke for the challenge and the enjoyment of getting to know the students.

I also enjoyed classes with the many juniors to whom I taught African American literature. I requested these classes partly because juniors were more mature and focused than freshmen or sophomores, and they didn't have one foot out the door like the seniors. More importantly, the curriculum was an engaging African American literature series of short stories, poetry, essays, and plays, which we loved reading and performing. Lorraine Hansberry's play, *A Raisin in the Sun*, prompted weeks of nearly full class participation with heartfelt dramatic readings and energizing discussions.

I taught 140 or so students each day, and it was difficult to get to know them all. Mrs. Rodino, who taught across the hall, gave me a great idea that stimulated their writing practice and taught me much about each student. Each week I assigned a topic for students to write about in their journals. They were given credit for the number of pages they wrote, not for their grammar or writing proficiency. They wrote and wrote and wrote without censorship. I learned so much about each student and used it to improve my teaching. I gave a bit of grammatical and spelling feedback at times, but mostly I offered personal responses to their writing. As a result, we developed much more personal relationships than we could achieve in class. I hope they knew that someone was listening to them every week — that I cared about them and was interested in their lives.

My students were educated beyond the official curriculum. I brought my political beliefs, actions, and activities into the classroom by showing slides and discussing the dangers of nuclear waste. I played the Marlo Thomas record *Free to Be You and Me*, hoping to provide an impetus for exploring equality between men and women, which was not yet an accepted value by many of my students.

We were a group of hard-working, idealistic, creative teachers, all eager to make a difference, but the chaos of the school system frequently thwarted good intentions and exhausted and discouraged teachers and students alike. Often my heart hurt as I contrasted all the privileges offered by my own high school in Evanston and the scarcity of resources for my students in Dorchester. Evanston Township High School had a natatorium with two swimming pools, acres of sports fields and a large football stadium, a well-equipped gymnastics space, a whole wing devoted to the theatre and musical arts with rehearsal rooms, and a luxurious auditorium with a professionally appointed stage and outstanding acoustics. It had a student guidance wing, modern science labs, a multi-room library, and an award-winning language curriculum where students could learn Japanese among many other languages.

And what did my students at the Burke have? The Burke had a decrepit auditorium with the majority of the seats broken and no playing fields or stadium or even one adequate gym. Nearly everything my high school had offered was either non-existent or substandard at the Burke, except for the teachers. The Burke had one guidance counselor, and the teacher's aides were assigned to hall monitor duty rather than classroom enrichment. Teachers received little training or support. My teaching supervisor gave me two important pieces of advice: "Use yellow chalk; it shows up better than white chalk" and "Wear sensible shoes."

The Boston neighborhoods were largely racially segregated and so were the schools. In 1972, the NAACP filed a lawsuit against the Boston School Committee with the stated goal of "equity in education regardless of race and class," which led to one of the most tumultuous times in Boston's history. In 1974, when Judge Arthur Garrity ordered school integration through busing, racial strife simmered over the impending news and the virulent resistance of whites to the prospect. Many students from the Columbia Point Housing Project in South Boston were bused to schools where they were most vehemently not wanted. They suffered extreme resistance and racist taunts in protest of their presence in previously all-white schools. These kids were among the least privileged — as were some of the white kids — ordered to be bused. Why did they not start integration in the very early grades and let the kids adjust to each other over time? I still remember the hatred against these good kids who were just doing what they were forced to do. Black kids, white kids, parents, and the whole community suffered from this busing.

Student absenteeism was high and income generally low. Students transferred in and out of school suddenly and frequently. Our principal always seemed a bit confused and even surprised that we were actually conducting classes on any particular school day.

How did the exhausted, stressed, hardworking, and eager teachers cope with the chaos of inner city teaching? We hung out together in our sacred refuge, the second floor teachers' room, every chance we got. It was a plain, narrow, high-ceilinged room with two tall windows at one end. We sat in straight-backed oak chairs at two sturdy oak tables set end to end that Miss Spencer had covered with contact paper. When worn out by the stress of teaching, we rested on the brown vinyl couch reminiscent of a psychiatrist's couch. We talked, laughed, and shared triumphs and discouragements including administrative nightmares. We got well acquainted with each other's lives, personalities, and teaching abilities, and supported each other through tough teaching days and personal difficulties.

After desegregation by busing, so many white students left the school system for private and parochial schools — or left the city altogether—that classes became extremely small. The students who stayed seemed depressed and unmotivated. The Boston Public Schools had hired many extra teachers—all non-white—in preparation for busing, but after a few years realized the schools were overstaffed. Previously, most of the teachers in the school system were white and the majority of students were not white. Therefore, six hundred white teachers were let go. I'd been there for ten years and was long tenured, but I was laid off too. It was hard to lose my job without a plan for what to do next, but I agreed with the decision to keep the non-white teachers employed. I lost a job, but gained lifelong friendships formed before I left.

We went through the trenches together at the Burke and stories of our teaching adventures and memorable students often enliven our conversations today, forty years later. Three of my former colleagues and I still get together for birthdays, holidays, and other outings. I wonder if another job could have given me such an intimate and supportive community. I was able to work with so many wonderful students, good people of intelligence and talent who deserved a great school system and yet persevered and often succeeded without one.

Growing Up and Good Times

FINDING HEAVEN IN
THE WOODS OF MAINE

Edy Rees

Every summer while I was growing up, we headed to Watson
Pond in Belgrade Lakes, Maine. My mother baked a pot of
beans. My father roasted a huge beef eye round in the rotis-
serie. They packed the car and tied the canoe to the top. Before the
Maine Turnpike was built, it took all of a very long day to reach our
destination. My sisters — Didi, Jane, and Marcia — and I passed the
time singing, playing games, reading, and napping. After exhaust-
ing every song and game we knew, we'd eventually fall asleep in
a heap in the back seat. Sometimes we took turns sleeping on the
floor, using the bump in the middle as a pillow, and the car robe
that hung across the back of the front seat as a blanket. We always
woke up when we reached Day's Store on Long Pond in Belgrade
Lakes, where we piled out of the car, yawning and stretching, and
ran inside to see the stuffed moose head, toy birch bark canoes, bal-
sam pillows, and other treasures. Our parents usually bought bread,
cheese, hamburger, venison, and homemade donuts. Then we made
the final leg of our journey up Route 27, turned left on Watson

Pond Road, and bumped slowly along a dusty, rutted dirt road until finally turning into Leon and Frances Watson's barnyard. After exchanging pleasantries, we drove down an even bumpier road to whichever cabin we were renting (for a song) that year. Once at the cabin, we often jumped out and ran, whooping and hollering, through the front door, out the pond-side door, down to the dock, and jumped into the pond fully clothed. We couldn't wait to revel in another visit to Maine.

At the age of six I taught myself to swim. My two older sisters, Jane and Didi, were already good swimmers. One day as they were horsing around with friends on the raft, I was getting bored, having been left alone with my pail and shovel on the nearby beach. So I devised a plan whereby I would walk out to the raft on the pond bottom, then pull myself up the anchor chain hand over hand, thus surprising the big kids by appearing on the raft — *voilá!* But as I kept trying to walk out there, it wasn't possible to stay under water because I kept bobbing to the surface. Finally, I realized I could actually swim by moving my arms and legs, so I dog-paddled out to the raft. The big kids had been so engrossed in their own water play that they never noticed my steady progress toward them until I arrived and triumphantly hauled myself onto the raft.

After I learned to swim, there was no stopping me. My friend Elise's mother had swum on Sweden's team in the Olympics. She taught all of my lake friends and me the classic crawl, the backstroke, the sidestroke, the butterfly stroke, and how to dive safely.

One dive revealed a sunken surprise when I was about eleven years old. A group of us had just discovered a high granite crag overlooking the deep water of a small cove hidden by hemlock and birch trees. We took turns diving off, spluttering to the surface, and climbing back up the rock to dive again, each time going a little deeper and opening our eyes to explore the cool depths of this unknown bottom. At some point, I saw something wrapped in burlap and swam back down to poke it with a stick. My friends joined me, and after a few of us had jabbed at this thing, it dislodged suddenly and floated to the surface, which immediately became covered with short brown fur, quickly spreading over most of the pond, and brought a sickening stench. Screaming, we scrambled out of the pond and ran to find Leon Watson, who drove down in his pickup truck and used a pitchfork to put the reeking carcass in the back. Leon confirmed it was a young female deer probably shot illegally by some hunter who then tried to hide his crime by wrapping her in burlap and sinking her with stones. The smell was so bad we had to evacuate for the rest of the day. By our return that evening the smell had abated, but there was still deer fur floating on the surface, and we stayed out of the water the next day until given the all clear that it was safe to swim again.

Leon and Frances Watson owned Watson Pond and several hundred surrounding acres, which included an apple orchard, barn, farmhouse, and huge vegetable and flower garden. In 1943, when my family first starting renting from the Watsons, there were just a handful of cabins. Those early renters so fell in love with the magic of this special place that they returned year after year, traveling from New York, New Jersey, Pennsylvania, and even farther away. We enthusiastic fans of Watson Pond became a tribe, keeping in touch, even visiting each other over the winter, and enjoying grand

ROSLINDALE

reunions back at the pond every summer. We also welcomed new families as Leon built additional cabins.

By the time I was ten, Leon had single-handedly built twelve rough-hewn log cabins, spaced out along one side of the secluded mile-long pond. For the first several years, there was no running water or electricity. We happily used the outhouse, rowed to the spring at the head of the pond to fill our bottles for drinking and cooking, hauled buckets of pond water for washing dishes, and bathed in the pond, using Ivory soap because it floated. To this day, the smell of Ivory soap carries me blissfully back to Watson Pond.

At some point, Leon installed inside toilets and a single water pipe from the pond to each kitchen sink. We still had to heat dishwater in the kettle on the wood-burning stove, where we did all our cooking and baking. Leon also wired each cabin for electricity, and then replaced the iceboxes on the back porches with real refrigerators.

Each cabin had a rowboat tied to a small dock, and my family also brought a canoe from home. Some families brought small sailboats. My father and I often went fishing together at dawn and dusk, proudly bringing home breakfast or dinner of trout, perch, bass, and pickerel. He taught me to troll, rowing very slowly and quietly, so as not to disturb the fish, and we took turns rowing and managing the rods. We both believed that whenever he lit his pipe one of us would get a nibble; this happened often enough to convince us it was true. He bought me my first good knife and taught me how to gut, clean, and scale our catch, rinsing everything on a special pond-side rock. It always amazed me how quickly the other wild creatures—birds, raccoons, etc.—feasted on the remains, leaving the rock spotless.

Edy with her children, Colin and Megan, at one of the Belgrade lakes

On the mornings when my dad and I didn't fish, I crept out of bed at first light, dressed quickly, and ran up the dirt road to the barn, where Leon and the farmhands let me help milk the cows, gather eggs, and brush Ike and Mamie (the team of gorgeous Clydesdales named after the President and his First Lady). Then the work crew insisted I join them for breakfast on the huge farmhouse porch, where we had steak, eggs, and amazing homemade donuts.

Later in the day after my friends were awake, we'd play in the hayloft, wildly swinging by a rope from one level to another. When it was haying time, Leon let us help, driving Ike and Mamie as they pulled the huge hay wagon. I loved jumping in the filling wagon to tamp down the hay and make room for more. Sometimes we kids made piles of peanut butter and jelly sandwiches, grabbed handfuls of comic books, and climbed the apple trees to spend a few blissful hours on a hot day. Then we raced back down the dirt road to the pond, found our bathing suits where they hung on the outside clotheslines, and met at the raft or at someone's dock for a swim and maybe our own version of water polo.

At least once a week during blueberry season, we rowed across the pond and climbed the long path to pick berries across the ridge we called Blueberry Hill. Entering that fragrant forest was stunning; it caused us to stop, take a deep breath, look around, and then smile as birdsong punctuated the hushed stillness. It took at least an hour to hike through the deep forest where sometimes we heard it begin to rain long before it penetrated the thick canopy of pine and hardwoods. Once we reached the berry fields on the second ridge, we filled our bellies and buckets with the sweetest, juiciest, tiniest Maine blueberries. Despite how many we ate while picking, we always brought back plenty for pies, pancakes, and putting on cereal.

As my sisters and I grew up, we kept returning to Watson Pond, bringing our own growing families. For the first twenty-eight years of my life, no matter what else was going on, I looked forward to that respite in the Maine woods. The last time I stayed at Watson Pond was during the summer of 1968, when my husband, his family, and several of our friends were there in August. My father-in-law had a shortwave radio on which we listened in horror to friends and allies being brutally beaten outside the Democratic National Convention in Chicago. But even that harsh real world intrusion couldn't obliterate the joy of being together at that enchanting pond. One night during our last visit, my friends Sally and Linda taught me the round "Dona Nobis Pacem" while we were paddling the canoe in the middle of the pond. As we sang, our voices echoed off Blueberry Hill, and we watched the Northern Lights and shooting stars over our heads in awe.

ROSLINDALE

In 1968 or '69, Leon and Frances sold off the pond and surrounding land and moved to Florida. We continued to return to the Belgrade Lakes area, to stay in other cabins on nearby ponds. The loons, black bears, bald eagles, and other precious wildlife still share their habitat with the few humans lucky enough to find their way to this sparkling slice of heaven.

THE PIRATES

John Mowles

I was brought up on McKone Street in the Neponset section of Dorchester during the 1930s and 1940s. McKone Street was fairly short and ran from Old Colony Boulevard (now Morrissey Boulevard) to Neponset Avenue close to the Quincy line. The street primarily consisted of two-and-a-half–story wood-frame structures with small backyards. Several houses had fruit trees on their properties. On Neponset Avenue was Herstack's Orchard, owned and cultivated by the Herstack family. It consisted of apple, sugar pear, and peach trees. If we gathered fruit from the ground, we were not challenged — but if we climbed the trees, we were chased off. We called it an orchard even through it was probably only the size of two house lots. Needless to say, during the early fall, a venture into a backyard or a jump off the Herstack's fence supplied us with ample snacks. On the corner of McKone Street and Neponset Avenue was Jarvis's Variety Store and across the street were Pop's Variety Store, Joe's Barbershop, and Brenennan's Meat Market, providing all the necessities of life. The Boston el trolley was our public transportation running from Neponset Circle to Fields Corner Station.

Growing up in Neponset, I hung out with ten or twelve kids of the same age on the street, not counting the girls. (We rarely played with girls.) We called ourselves a "gang" but not in the context of what is now a gang. We were just a bunch of guys hanging out. And we called ourselves the Pirates. As we grew older, the gang expanded as we migrated to adjacent streets. I don't remember anyone having a real individual close friendship. It was more "all for one and one for all." We played sports, got into trouble, and generally hung together through our early youth.

We played a lot of street games, including "lady" (touch) football in which the so-called "ball" was made of a rolled-up newspaper and tape. We played street hockey (yeah, with a real puck) and "half-ball," which we played with a tennis ball cut in half and a broomstick for a bat. Half-ball consisted of two players to a team, a pitcher and a catcher. In some foreign areas — such as New York — it was called stickball. Garvey Playground was also our field for pickup baseball and football games. In those days there was no Little League or Pop Warner football.

We were, for the most part, able to play in the street uninterrupted by autos as only two or three families on the street had cars. Any time a car would interrupt our game, we would wave to those we knew. If it was a stranger, we would boo them. All of our street games were played on the lower end of the street where there were a lot of vacant lots, because we knew we wouldn't disturb the neighbors. The sidewalks were of common cement and curbstones, and I remember that on the lower end where we played, the weeds and tall stocks would grow between the walk and the curb. By the end of summer, there was a wall of weeds along the sidewalk.

McKone Street, Neponset Gang.
Front row, left to right: Charlie
Mooney, Jim McGrail, Bill Flynn.
Back row, left to right: Charlie
Lyons, Sonny Parotta, Bunso
Byrnes, Ed Devine, Joe Sullivan.

Across the street from my house there was a large wooded lot we called the "Rockies." We would play in these woods, building forts and tree houses, and playing war games. We would also pretend to camp out by building a fire in a small hole where we would bake potatoes. Sad to say, construction took the Rockies away from future generations of kids.

Ice hockey and skating had a short season because—unlike today—we didn't have skating rinks. There was a sunken marsh behind the Garvey Park playground that local firemen would flood by opening a fire hydrant, and a steady low temperature was needed for it to freeze. Hockey games were occasionally cancelled because of soft ice. In summer, we had better luck with swimming. We lived a ten-minute walk from Tenean Beach so, as you can imagine, our summer days were spent there. We were off to the beach by 8:00 A M, then home for lunch, and back to the beach.

The Neponset Gang, 2012 (left to right): John Mowles, Bill MacLeod, Paul Joyce, and Bill Flynn

In the late afternoon and early evening, our gang would hang out at Pop's. I say we hung out in the early evening because when the streetlights came on you had better be home, or else. At one point we all wore scally caps to look like wise guys, which was probably not a good idea. Once when the woman across the street called the cops, we ran away but were easily identified by our hats.

Our gang started to break up when we attended different high schools and formed new friendships. Everyday contact also dwindled because of the time spent with girlfriends, part-time jobs, and other life adventures, but we still managed to hang out occasionally.

After high school, our gang completely separated. We all enlisted in different branches of the armed services during the Korean War. I joined the navy and over a period of three years I ran into a few old chums at different navy bases including Bill Flynn in Cuba, Bill MacLeod in Newport, Carl Nash in New York, and others in various parts of the world.

Our friendships were renewed after the Korean War, but we could not get together as often because of jobs and marriages. We would see each other as a group only at weddings, reunions, and funerals. After retirement, I started to spend more time with four childhood pals. We meet several times a year. We all had successful careers: Joe Sullivan was a bank president; Bill MacLeod was also a bank president; Paul Joyce was a medical supply executive; Bill Flynn worked for the Boston Edison Company; and I was a detective captain in the Massachusetts State Police. These days we meet with wives and lady friends present, and the conversation consists of families and grandchildren and the like. Inadvertently, the conversation almost always reverts to our childhood escapades. Gone are the Rockies, the vacant lots we played in, the trolley cars, the gas streetlights, and many friends. Although time moves on, our memories remain and will until the end.

MY FATHER'S GIFT TO ME

Mary A. McCarthy

Sunday mornings when Dad shaved we joined him — my sister, my brother, and I. We were three, four, and five years old respectively. We lined up next to the sink and watched his every move.

He opened the medicine chest, took out a cream-colored mug with a small brush hanging on the side. The brush had a yellow and black handle and soft tan bristles. It was clean as a whistle. His razor was long and shiny. He opened it with a very slow and careful gesture, and placed it on the edge of the sink next to the mug. It was different from a knife in shape but was as sharp as a knife, so Dad said. The dark brown leather strap for sharpening the razor hung on the wall by a shiny metal hook next to the mirror and down to the side of the sink. When all of the equipment was out and in its place on the sink, Dad turned on the hot water, cupped his hands, and wet his face — just enough, not too much. He took a small hand towel from the rack and placed it on his left shoulder.

We were silent. We knew what would happen next and the anticipation began.

He took the yellow-handled brush in hand, wet it under the running water, and dipped it into the mug. As he began to lather the brush we wiggled with excitement. He swirled the brush around in the shaving cream until the bubbles rose above the edge of the mug. We could see them. I could almost feel them. Then he began to apply those bubbles to his face and neck. What a sight. He looked like Santa Claus, but even better.

And then it was time.

He leaned down and, with brush in hand, he lathered those lovely bubbles and creamy soap on my cheeks and chin. It felt warm and smooth and it tickled too. He then did the same for my brother and sister. The silence was broken. We were giggling and squirming.

Dad returned the brush to its place inside the mug and the mug to the side of the sink. Slowly and methodically, he picked up his razor and started the rhythmic stroking of razor on leather strap — sharpening.

We fell back to quiet and Dad began to hum, which he always did as he worked around the house. He lifted the shiny blade and began his shave, always on his right cheek near his ear. He pushed the blade down his cheek with a scraping sound, and the cream piled against it. He washed the blade clean under the slow running water, wiped it dry on the towel on his shoulder, and lifted the blade again to the place right next to the last stroke. Again the scraping sound, the pile

The five McCarthy children (John, Mary Ann, Henry, Helen, and Daniel) all lined up once again…this time for a photo!

of soapy cream against the blade, and again washed clean. After three or four strokes he would set the razor on the sink.

It was time. It was my turn.

Dad would lean down and with his first finger pressed against my cheek he would shave those lovely bubbles off my face, stroke after stroke. His left hand cupped my chin to be sure he did a fine job. I didn't move. Then he went on to my brother, then my sister. He continued—humming, stroking, rinsing—until all the bubbles were gone. He filled the sink with warm water and held each of us in turn so we could wash our faces. We got our own face cloth wrapped around our cheeks and chin. We were thrilled.

I don't remember how often we did this. It was wartime. Dad worked at the Charlestown Navy Yard and his shift varied. But this I do know: when we joined Dad in his shaving ritual, it was delightful.

Yes, I loved to watch my father shave, to knot his tie and pull it tight to his collar, to button his vest and attach his watch chain then slip the watch into its small pocket. Dad had such respect for and attention to everyday activities. He honored all that he did. We lined up to wash our hands or brush our teeth or get on our jackets, hats, and mittens to go for a walk with him on Sunday after dinner. We hummed, too.

I still hum as I work around the house today.

This was my father's gift to me.

ON SPORTS

Judith Klau

Wellesley College, 1956. Dressed in the requisite bloomer and tunic, my friend—the late, adorable Sheila Mahoney—and I are playing volleyball to fulfill the hated physical education requirement. (We also learned quoits and shuffleboard, to prepare us for our inevitable future life aboard yachts.) The elastic-leg bloomers and the button-down tunic were made of the kind of cotton that today one finds in hospital scrubs. Their color was possibly the only ugly shade of blue ever invented. Sheila and I are deeply engaged in discussing our dates for the following weekend when the ball heads for us and drops to the ground. We pay it no heed. We continue to talk and are headed back to the gym when two large and very angry young women confront us, accusing us of having lost the game for our side. They tell us threateningly to meet them outside after the showers. They march off, and Sheila and I look at each other in horror. Of a single mind, we scramble on our hands and knees up the nearly vertical hill behind the gym and run to the safety of our rooms in the dormitory at the top. Those scars on my legs are from the brambles.

127

A hundred years later, I am teaching at one of the country's best-known preparatory schools and have finally developed the understanding that sports, when properly and generously taught, give girls great pleasure and fine skills. A generous impulse drives me to donate my forty-year-old wedding dress—residue of an unsuccessful marriage but a beautiful dress nonetheless—to the drama program for a production that requires such a costume. I am not now, was not then, and never have been a slim person, but I was amazed to find that the dress would not fit anyone at the school, including the fifteen-year-old who was supposed to wear it, because the waist was considerably too small. Why? Because they had all participated in sports and had developed their *latissimus dorsi* muscles ("lats" to you) in ways that we wasp-waisted beauties of 1957 never had.

Sports do change us in ways that mark us forever.

A DREAM FULFILLED

Sandy Kilbride

When I was very young, my dad would take me to see old silent films in the basement of the Sacred Heart Church in the North End, and to the larger theaters to see major movies. I'm not sure how old I was when I saw my first major movie, *Snow White and the Seven Dwarfs,* but I do recall being very frightened by the wicked queen.

My father worked for the company that printed the *Playbill* for many of the theater productions in Boston and was given passes to plays as I was growing up. When I was a teenager my mom and dad took me to my first play, *The Merry Widow,* which was really an operetta. I remember the music and dancing and how much I enjoyed it as I began to develop an appreciation for the theater.

I also loved movies and, like many young girls in those days, I wanted to be a movie star. My friends and I often pretended that we were leading actors. By age ten or eleven, we were putting on plays for our families in the basement playroom of my home in Brighton, where we had moved when I was six.

When finally I was old enough to go to the movies with my friends, we went to the nearby theater known then as the Egyptian, located in Brighton Center. Designed with an Egyptian motif, exotic decor with statues in the huge foyer, balcony and loge seating, it accommodated an audience of 1,700. I loved that theater. I spent many Saturdays there watching cowboy movies and cartoons. Sunday afternoons were for the really big movies, usually two features with newsreels in between, all for twenty-five cents. Many times we spent the entire afternoon there, and on the way home went into our pretend mode after deciding who would portray which role we had just watched. Oh, how I loved those walks home.

In my teen years, Friday nights became my movie night at the Egyptian, sometimes with my girlfriends and sometimes with a boyfriend, with a soda or ice cream afterward at the local hangout, the Puritan Coffee Shop.

I went to Mount St. Joseph Academy in high school. The school did not have a theater program, but the senior class always produced a play. In 1953, my senior year, the play was *Pride and Prejudice*. Throughout my high school years I hadn't really stood out in any way. I was not outgoing. I lacked confidence and was only an average student. But I thought that this play was my chance to do something outstanding, to act and be on stage for my family and fellow classmates to see. Although I looked forward with trepidation to auditions, I decided to try out for the part of Jane.

The reading of the scene would be a few short lines when Jane received news that the man who had expressed interest in her had left without a word and wouldn't be back. I was sure I could feel that

The Egyptian Theatre, Brighton-Allston Historical Society

emotion of betrayal and would be capable of shedding a few tears. As I watched the others who went ahead of me, I started to sweat, and butterflies crept in as I tried to remember how I rehearsed at home the night before. I was aching to be in this play. Then it was my turn. I could feel my nerves jumping as I walked to the stage. I went over to Mrs. Bennett, who was sitting on a chair, and dropped to my knees in front of her. With a few sobs I blurted out, "It's over, entirely over; he won't return and I must accept it."

Boy, I did it, and I surprised myself with my reading. I felt sure I had some talent and would get the part because of the compliments I received. But the next tears I shed were in disappointment over not getting chosen. The reason, I was told, was that my part-time job after school would keep me from rehearsals. This was quite a letdown for a young, impressionable girl when I was never even given the choice of giving up my job in order to be in the show.

Decades passed before my next audition.

My husband and I moved to Hawaii when my youngest child was five years old. After a couple of years there, I enrolled him in a youth theater program as an after-school activity, with the hope that he would appreciate theater. He seemed to enjoy being in plays and meeting other kids. It also gave me a chance to be active behind the scenes. I volunteered to monitor the kids, work with the costume department and help out with stage management. From time to time, I was asked to be on stage when the scene required some adults, and had a few lines here and there as well as some singing parts.

Eventually my son lost interest in theater. This presented me with a choice: go on volunteering or pursue my own acting ambitions. That summer, I auditioned with the Maui Community Theater. I didn't know at the time that quite a few people involved with this community theater program had moved to Hawaii from California, where they had acted. If I had, I may have thought twice before I went up against that competition when I auditioned for *On Golden Pond*. I did the reading and was told again that it was good, but once again I didn't get the part, this time because I was too ethnic looking. All the chosen cast members looked Anglo-Saxon and this play, highlighting a family, required the actors to look alike. Wow, I never thought my Italian heritage would be a hindrance in landing a part. How naïve. Another letdown, but as an adult I wasn't nearly as affected. I was disappointed but not devastated.

I enrolled in a community college theater class that offered instruction in acting, directing, and producing plays. The students chose the play, auditioned, cast the actors, built the sets, co-directed,

133

and managed the production. The play we selected was *A Streetcar Named Desire*. I won a bit part as the beggar woman selling flowers in the street, but I got so much more out of the experience that it was a total delight in every way. I not only learned about acting and all the parts that go into a play production, but I also worked with new people, enjoyed the camaraderie, shared the fun times and the challenges, created costumes and built sets, and — not to be forgotten — celebrated the after-party.

My first major role was as Willy Loman's wife in *Death of a Salesman* at the Maui Community Theater. That was a big step for me. All the little-girl shyness and fears were gone, and I finally had the opportunity to showcase my ability as an actor.

Linda Loman had a great burden. Her husband was losing it, her sons were at odds, and one son had little use for his father. She had to play the balancing act between father and son and explain Willy's predicament to them. "Willy Loman never made a lot of money. His name was never in the paper. He's not the finest character that ever lived. But he's a human being and a terrible thing is happening to him. So attention must be paid. He's not to be allowed to fall into his grave like an old dog. Attention, attention must be finally paid to such a person."

Here was a man who worked hard his whole life as a salesman on the road, who put so much hope in his sons' futures and was disappointed in the result. His life was going downhill, and when he finally realized that he himself couldn't do any better, he wanted to end his life and leave his family with the insurance money. The play is depressing, especially in the final scene when Linda Loman, totally

Sandy acting in Death of a Salesman

exhausted, delivers her monologue at the cemetery. "Willy, I made the last payment on the house today. Today, dear. And there'll be nobody home. We're free and clear. We're free. We're free."

A sense of sadness filled the theater. People left with heavy hearts and maybe a few tears. I decided then and there that the roles I would play would be in comedy. I wanted to make people laugh and leave the theater feeling good.

I continued acting and have had lead roles in plays such as *Beyond Therapy, Fiddler on the Roof,* Neil Simon's *Brighton Beach Memoirs* and *Fools,* among others. This community theater group was fortunate to have wonderful set builders, and one set I was quite fond of was my house in Brighton Beach. While building the set, I added some of my own props from home, and even used a few of my dresses to hang on the clothesline out back. We referred to the set as "Sandy's house," and I had such an attachment to that set that I was reduced to tears when we had to strike it at the close of the show. I had to learn to let go.

135

My grown children lived close by in Maui and attended many of my performances, but my parents never had seen one of my plays. They were back in Brighton, and although they visited often, never when I was involved in the theater. A couple of years after I quit doing shows, I received a call from a teacher/director of a private high school. She was producing *Brighton Beach Memoirs* and the senior student playing the role of the mom had taken ill. Since I knew the part, she asked if I would fill in. I told her that I was available.

Now you might think that doing this play for a second time would be a breeze. However, working with seasoned actors is quite different from doing a show with high school students, some of whom had no previous experience. Should you happen to drop a line or two, there was very little help from the others on stage with you. I recall having a memory lapse during a particular scene where I was on stage with two others. Since they hadn't a clue how to respond to me, I spent several agonizing moments trying to recall my line while I walked around the set doing business until my memory came back and I was able to continue with my lines. I can still feel the anxiety that created. Fortunately, no one in the audience noticed. The teacher/director was great. In fact, she had been the director of the play, *On Golden Pond*, the one in which I did not get cast.

The great thing about doing this student play was that my parents were visiting at the time, and although I never became a professional actor, in one way I was fulfilling a childhood dream of performing on stage in front of them. Finally, the last time I ever performed, my parents got to see their daughter in a high school play.

THE NEIGHBORHOOD

Patricia Geary

When I was a child, my world was a block of six houses. All of the houses were two stories—one floor for the owner and the other a rental. My parents purchased our gray-shingled home in 1938, the year I was born. At that time, we lived on the first floor. My father worked at the Hood Rubber Company in Watertown and my mother stayed home with the kids. I was the third oldest in a family of seven, five girls and two boys. Three sisters rented the second floor. To help pay the rent, they sublet one bedroom with a bathroom and kitchen privileges to the Neals, a young, newly married, interracial couple. Mr. Neal used to play with us after work. He had nicknames for all of us—Princess and Sluggo are two that I remember.

Jump rope, hide and seek, tag, hopscotch, and red rover were some of the games we played. A rope, chalk, and imagination were all that was needed to entertain us. We also played with our cousins, one girl and three boys, who were similar ages. We weren't allowed to play at other childrens' houses. After school, we would walk home with our cousins and safely go past the big kids.

Our backyard was adjacent to our cousins' yard and we shared a common fence and gate. This made it easier for my mother and Aunt Margaret to watch out for us. We had a clothesline that ran between the two houses. Every washday, our laundry hung out to dry on the line. On winter days, the sheets used to come in as stiff as boards and had to be heated in the kitchen before folding. My mother and aunt used to have regular conversations from opposite ends of the clotheslines.

After one winter storm, we decided to build a snow slide with our cousins. We shoveled the snow up against the back porch high enough to reach the ledge. We piled snow along the house to the side fence and around to the next section of fence. To us, the slide was enormous — about five feet tall at the top and three feet tall along the fence, and it extended about ten to fifteen yards. We launched ourselves from the porch and flew around the corner landing in the fresh snow. When it was cold enough, we would pour water on the slide to ice it up and make it even faster. It was a magnificent snow slide.

We had a front yard with a border hedge and beds of flowers, and the backyard was where my mother had her vegetable garden. When we were very young, we had a chicken coop with four chickens under the porch. My mother, having grown up on a farm in Ireland, brought the country to our backyard when she arrived home one day with those chickens. They were black and brown, and did a lot of cackling. The four oldest children chose their favorites. There were a few good egg layers and one not so good. My brother used to get up early and go out to the coop to search for eggs for his breakfast. Over the year, one by one, those chickens disappeared. As a child, I never understood where they had gone.

Living on one side of our house was a German couple, Mr. and Mrs. Albig. They owned their brown two-family house and were friendly but reserved. They had two cocker spaniels, Maggie and Fritz. Mrs. Albig grew a large vegetable garden in her backyard with potatoes, carrots, lettuce, tomatoes, rhubarb, and many other vegetables that were unfamiliar to me. There were gooseberry bushes growing on our shared fence that we were allowed to pick and eat. She also had strawberries and raspberries. You could usually hear Mrs. Albig coming as she wore garden clogs on her feet that made a distinctive clip-clop sound. After Mr. Albig died, it didn't seem very long before Mrs. Albig had a new husband. She was then Mrs. Itner.

The neighbors on our other side, the McGoverns, were Irish. Their son, John, was a coalman and their daughter, Mary (called Marion), was a teacher. Every Christmas Eve, Marion would arrive and leave a bag of presents for us. I didn't realize until much later that she had done this for all of the children in her family as well as for our cousins and us. Some of my favorite gifts were a doll, puzzles, and books. She never gave knitted hats, scarves, or mittens. I remember the feeling of actually owning a book. We had encyclopedias at home that we used for school projects, but to have my own books to read was very special to me. John married Nonie, who came from Dingle, Ireland. They lived on the first floor. His coal truck was parked in their driveway between our two houses. My mother never had to worry about running out of fuel; John made sure of this.

Across the street from the Itners were the O'Connors, a young English war bride, her soldier husband, and a son. This was the only neighbors' house that I can remember going into as a child. We would play with baby Tommy and chat with Mrs. O'Connor. I have a fond memory of Mrs. O'Connor repairing her nylons with needle and thread. She had a basket on the floor containing her nylons that had "ladders." She took many pictures of Tommy and us with her Brownie camera, and later a moving film camera.

Across the street was a house owned by a Syrian family of five, the Cahalys. We used to play with their daughter Caroline who was my age. Mr. Cahaly owned a convenience store not too far away on Franklin Street. When my sister was a baby, she drank some kerosene from a bottle that had been left outside during the painting of our house. My mother was frantic. Mr. Cahaly rushed out of his house and took them in his car to the hospital. These were the kind of neighbors we had.

The Steeles lived across from the McGoverns. Mr. Steele was a sulky racer down at the Charles River Speedway, which was at the end of Everett Street in Allston. A sulky is a two-wheeled horse-drawn buggy with a small seat for the driver. Their grandson, Victor, lived on the first floor of the Itners house, and we used to go with him down to watch the races and to visit the horses in their stables. The smell of manure was something I'll never forget. I am not a country girl!

There was a drugstore at the end of our street run by the pharmacist, Bill Coviello, and his wife. Their pharmacy window was in the

The Family, 1948. Back row: Robert, Patricia, Margaret, Edward. Front row: Eileen, Anne, Joan.

back of the store; it was a place where neighbors would fill prescriptions and consult with the pharmacist rather than going to a doctor. The drugstore had everything a child could want—Milky Way bars, sodas, frappes, banana splits, sundaes, and of course penny candy. As you came in, there was a soda fountain on the right with stools surrounding it. On the shelves were various glasses for each concoction. It wasn't often that I had enough money to actually order something. However, when I had earned some money babysitting or by running errands, I would spend it at the drugstore. I loved their root beer floats—a tall glass of root beer with a scoop of vanilla ice cream, a straw, and a long spoon.

The penny candy area was in the rear of the store near the pharmacy. For five cents, you could select enough candy to fill a small paper bag. I remember pondering over the candy window — decisions, decisions. Root beer barrels, pink candy dots on paper, pink bubblegum, red and black licorice, and bullseyes were many of my favorites. Mr. and Mrs. Coviello were so patient with us, which must have been difficult.

One time the store held a contest. You just had to fill in your name and address for the chance to win a prize. I was playing at home when my brother came running up to me, "You've won a prize!" We ran to the drugstore, where I discovered that my name was on the posted winner's page and that I had won a shiny new pair of roller skates. This was a skate that clipped on to your shoes and had a key to regulate the size. I was thrilled, never having won anything before. I remember flying down the street on those skates. A year or so later, as the fad for scooters hit Brighton, my cousins and I took the skates apart and attached them to wooden boxes from the grocer to become scooters.

My neighborhood was probably not unique, but to me it was an exciting place in which to grow up. There were always children playing. Today, our family is the only one that remains from that era. All the others have died or moved away. The houses have been modernized. There are more cars on the street and in the driveways, but no sounds of children playing in the street. In the blink of an eye, however, I can transport myself back to the wonderful time we had growing up there.

HAPPY TRAILS

Claire Banatt

I took a job at Eastman Kodak right out of high school. My mother was in the hospital, having suffered a complete break-down, which is what they called it at the time. My father wanted me to stay home to take care of the house and get the meals, but my guidance counselor at school had some different ideas for me. She set up an appointment for an interview at Eastman Kodak when it was on Bromfield Street in Boston. I went to see a Mr. Homeier, or his secretary Miss Reynolds. I must have passed the interview, because I lasted seven years there.

After my first year there, I met Marie. She is a year younger so she started the year after I did. She came from East Boston and I came from Hyde Park. Marie used the bookkeeping machine, which looked like an oversized typewriter, while I took dictation, and mostly typed invoices. My boss was named Mr. Ryan. He must not have been too bad, because I visited with Marie on the other side of the office quite frequently. Marie had brown hair and it was natu-rally curly. I was always envious of her in that regard. She always had a smooth way of walking. No bouncing up and down. She has a very pretty face, with a delicate nose and blue eyes.

We started to go dancing together. We called it stag dancing, as we went without partners and we would always come home together. On Wednesdays and Saturdays I would meet her in town, or in Forest Hills, depending on our destination. We went to the Hotel Vendome in Back Bay, or Moseley's On the Charles in Dedham, or the City Club. We knew all the dance halls. There was a place over on Revere Beach Parkway that had about three dance floors. There were some good dancers there, especially Moseley's. Talk about dancing with the stars.

Moseley's is still a dance hall. It is just one floor, and at the door when you bought your ticket you would go to the right to the ladies' room and to the left would be the coat check. Right ahead was the dance floor and the bandstand. When we went, Don Dudley was playing our favorite tunes. After we would check ourselves out in the ladies' room, we would go all the way to the end of the ballroom and wait to be asked to dance. We had to have a pleasant smile on our faces and have a look of expectancy.

We loved to dance. Once, I remember dancing with a fellow from Framingham who was a policeman. He came all that way just to dance, and what a dancer he was. We went whirling around that dance floor in nothing flat. We did sambas, rumbas, waltzes, as well as foxtrots. We even tried the black bottom, a dance popular in the 1920s. One Christmas, we sang in a choral group with Don Dudley's band at Moseley's. Don said that if anyone was off-key, he would drown us out with the brass. One of the songs I remember we sang was "Mr. Sandman."(Many years later I met a priest who grew up in West Roxbury. He mentioned Moseley's only to say that his father always steered him away from going there, as it was only "riffraff" who went there. Well, I beg to differ.)

Marie and I didn't just go dancing together; we also vacationed together. One year Marie and I made reservations for Mont Tremblant in Montreal. I was never on such a long train ride in all my life. We went through Vermont and on and on. On the trip we didn't see much snow, but they assured us at the hotel that there would be snow. Well, there wasn't. We went bike riding the whole week. It wasn't so bad. We got a chance to meet some Royal Mounties who were also staying there. They were pretty impressive. Their uniforms reminded me of that song, "When I'm Calling You" from the movie *Indian Love Call*, starring Jeannette MacDonald and Nelson Eddy. We also met a couple of young girls from New York State who Marie kept in touch with for a while. There was delicious food and a wonderful sparkling wine.

We went back the next year and we did get to go skiing. There was a little slope in back of the hotel. It was called a little Alp. We took lessons in side-stepping and the herringbone technique to get uphill on skis. We also learned to snowplow. From there we got gradually into putting weight on the downhill ski, which is the key to successful skiing. We took a lot of tumbles. Marie took to it better than I did. I was a little jealous. She got to go on the higher hills.

We belonged to the Snow Chasers, which was a ski club in Lynn. I would stay at Marie's house Friday night and we'd go to meet or to be picked up by another skier looking for someone to carpool and help pay for the trip to the ski area. We loved going to ski in Maine or New Hampshire. We would ski for the day and come home, or stay overnight somewhere and ski on Sunday, too.

Marie sometimes had trouble keeping her weight down. I can remember her coming to work with a grapefruit for lunch, the latest weight-reduction fad. But during ski season, she always slimmed down to a very lovely figure. She should have had skiing in her life constantly.

I was never as good at skiing as Marie. One winter, I broke my ankle while on a trip to Cannon Mountain, in New Hampshire, north of Concord. They sent me to the closest hospital and I had to stay there for a week. I'll never forget how Marie sent a book to me to read, a book by A.J. Cronin, who was popular at the time. I thought that was so nice of her. I could tell she put a lot of thought into the type of book she sent. At the end of the week, my brother and brother-in-law came to get me. They packed me into an old car and it had two flat tires during the trip back to Boston.

My boss at the time, Mr. Ryan, was quite perturbed that I would be out of work for so long. I had to stay home for eleven weeks in all. That bone just didn't want to heal. After I left the company, they told me that Mr. Ryan broke his ankle tripping over a hassock. Fate was getting back at him.

Marie was always very outgoing. When we went on vacation she would always be the one to introduce herself to others, and as a result we got to know a lot of people. She also loved to take charge. She was the one to plan the vacations and I went along. She influenced me in many ways. For example, she says what is on her mind and asks other people for their opinions so that she can find a consensus. By her example, she taught me to include people in my plans.

We had such a great time skiing and dancing and meeting new people. It was at the City Club in Boston where I met Ed. The City Club had dancing in one room and drinking in another. I don't remember if there was a band or a disc jockey. We danced on the second floor where everyone stood around a semi-circle and the dance floor was a sunken affair. Ed approached and asked me to dance and he was a pretty good dancer, but he also made me laugh with his jokes. I guess my laughter encouraged him, so he asked me to go and eat after the dance. At my suggestion, we went to Chinatown. I thought, "Doesn't everyone like Chinese food?" Apparently not. Ed tried to order a breakfast of toast and eggs, and the waiter was flummoxed. "Breakfast?" he asked. "Go to Hayes Bickford's," which is what it was called in those days. So we did, and I missed out on Chinese food that night. But Ed and I have been married for all these years. He has since learned to love Chinese food.

Ed and I got married in 1965 and after a few years, Marie met and married Phil. Marie and Phil never had children, but I had four. She would still keep in touch and invite me to her parties. They threw the best parties, especially at Halloween. We dressed up in our costumes, and Marie and Phil always had games planned that were hilarious. They had us all laughing so much we were in tears, which was just what we needed after stressful days taking care of kids. One of the games consisted of behaving like a mouse, squeaks and all, looking for a prize (cheese). Watching grown-ups down on their hands and knees saying "squeak, squeak" just hit the funny bone. One year Ed dressed up as a cat and went around purring and rubbing his cheeks on everyone. Oh, he was in his glory.

Marie was a leader, even in her married life. Marie and Phil loved to sail, so Ed and I learned to sail. They bought a boat and we rented one and we went on lots of trips up the east coast. They bought an RV, so we got an RV. They drove theirs all over the country, even to Alaska. We drove ours to visit our adult kids. So, in a way Marie was still leading me on adventures. We're still good friends, although we aren't as active as we once were. These days, we go out to dinner and sit for a couple of hours and chat. She has shared every phase of my adult life, every adventure I've had. Think what I would have missed if I hadn't gone out for that first job interview in high school.

Women's Work

AN EDUCATED WOMAN

Raven Elliott

In my family, going to college was like going to grammar school. It was expected. Going to school every day and learning and doing your homework were as common as eating. I was born in Greensboro, North Carolina. My father, a dentist, was educated at Howard University in Washington, D.C. My mother attended Fisk University in Nashville, Tennessee. She was a high school English teacher at Palmer Memorial Institute, in Sedalia, North Carolina. Palmer was a private school for "colored" children started in 1902 by Charlotte Hawkins Brown. Daddy had been married previously, but his first wife died leaving him with two children to raise, a boy and a girl, Alex and Doris. All five of us lived in Greensboro, where my daddy practiced dentistry and mama stopped teaching to be with us.

The house where we lived in Greensboro had no basement. In this way it was like all the other homes there. They were two-story homes in which the furnace burned coal and was in the kitchen next to the stove. This was in the 1920s. One night my brother went into the yard to get more coal and saw that the house was on fire. He came back in the house yelling, "Get out! The house is on fire!" He continued shouting, "Call the fire department!" He said this even as he was running to the phone.

I was upstairs asleep. He shouted, "Get Raven!" to our sister, who ran upstairs to wake me. At that time, we always had a babysitter who lived with us. She was a student at Bennett College, a girls' school, a few blocks from us. She ran for the phone to call the fire trucks. I still have a very vivid picture of rubbing my eyes to wake up. My sister wrapped me in a blanket and we walked hurriedly down the stairs and out the front door as the fire trucks came clanging down the street. My sister was not much taller than I was, but she took care of me, holding my hand all the way. The sitter ran to the street and yelled to the firemen, pointing to our house. Mom and Dad had gone to a movie. They got home as fast as they could, hearing there was a fire at the house. Everything was okay, thank goodness; there was just some damage to the roof.

Our family had to get away from the racism in the South. My daddy was a dentist and was also a political activist, an "upstart." He helped spread the word about a man who was nominated to the Supreme Court by Herbert Hoover in Washington D.C. This man had a shady past in terms of his statements about Negroes as having limited value as voters. My father climbed over the transom of the local newspaper to deliver published accounts of these statements to Walter White, then president of the NAACP and a family friend. With my daddy's efforts, that evidence was used to mobilize political pressure nationally to stop the nomination.

After that, we had to move away from Greensboro, for fear of being killed. The family left North Carolina, a home to generations of my people. My mom, sister, and I lived with my Aunt Raven, my namesake, in Atlantic City for a year while Daddy began to establish a new dental practice in Yonkers. My mom's sister, like my mother, was also a teacher. During the year, one of my seventh grade classmates was Adolph Elliott and I got a crush on him. He had a girlfriend so I didn't make any headway with him at first. But by the end of the year, we were close friends.

Adolph was born in Charleston, South Carolina, and then his family moved to Atlantic City, near his favorite uncle Joe. After his mother's death, he moved to Jamaica, New York, to live with Hattie. She was a real good friend of his aunt in Charleston. He called her Aunt Hattie, because she became like a mother to him. He moved around the same time as my family reunited the following year in Yonkers.

Adolph and I continued to see each other over the years. He would ride his bike to the subway from Jamaica, Long Island. Carrying his bike, he then had to catch the streetcar to Yonkers to visit me and have dinner with my mother and father. On dates, we would take the ferry across the Hudson and take long walks in the Palisades Park in New Jersey. To get back home, Daddy would drive Adolph and his bike to the subway, to save him the streetcar fare. After the subway got to Long Island, he would ride his bike back home. After all that, I knew he really wanted to see me.

After high school graduation, I went to Fisk University in Nashville, where my mother and aunt had gone to school. I wanted to study chemistry. I lived in the dormitory and, like everybody else there, it really was the first time being away from home. It seemed like everybody learned to smoke right away, except for me. I was a very stubborn individual, and I was never one who would just follow what was being done. I made up my mind. I decided that I wasn't going to smoke until my sophomore year, which I did. While at Fisk, I was on the tennis team and was an active Alpha Kappa Alpha. I'm still in touch by phone with one of the girls who was my first-year roommate in college.

Across the street from Fisk was Meharry Medical College, and that's where I did my graduate work in biochemistry. There I went to school with people who would become doctors and nurses. Many girls at Fisk were sent to college or went to college to find husbands and were disappointed when these doctors' wives came to their graduation. Many hearts were broken. But I was sent to Fisk to get an education. I did research at Meharry and helped teach biochemistry classes to future doctors and nurses. And I met someone at Meharry, Hyland, a dental student, and dated him until graduation.

After I got my master's degree, I moved back to Yonkers to live with Mom and Dad. When Adolph got out of the army, he came to Yonkers to visit me and my family. At that time, I was ready to get a job in the field of chemistry and get married, I thought, to my friend Hyland. But, when Adolph came back to visit, that changed my mind about a future husband. I wanted Adolph, not Hyland.

After that, I was ready to move again. I wanted to find my own job, not one that my parents found for me. So I moved to Detroit to live with my sister, Doris, and her husband "Flute" Burgess. Adolph came to visit me, got a job, began college in Detroit, and we got engaged and married in Doris' front room. We lived with them for a while and then bought our own house right behind theirs. Adolph worked in the post office and then took a job with the civil service. "Biff" was the nickname I gave him because "Adolph" was the name of the dog in the comic strip *Dinglehoofer und His Dog Adolph* about a German-American immigrant and his beloved dog. It was a very popular comic strip in the 1920s and 1930s.

After we got married in 1946, I was working at the hospital lab where my sister worked, and thought that could be a good career. She felt I should go elsewhere because people were very isolated when they worked in those settings. Confidentiality of patient information was a major concern, so people working in those basement labs had a hard time getting to know other people in the hospital. So when the opportunity came up, I moved on with a job at Ford Motor Company working in the Carver Lab, Mr. Ford's private laboratory. The way I got the job was through Ford's butler, Mr. Foster, who knew my sister. We didn't know him as a butler. To us, he was a nice man we met in church. When I was hired, I was the only African American employee, and one of only three women in the lab. People that worked in Mr. Ford's lab had to be known by him. Mr. Foster knew that Ford needed a technician in the lab and scientists for research; because of his contact with him, I got the job.

I researched soybeans. Ford had been impressed with George Washington Carver at Tuskegee and wanted to make products from soybeans as Carver had made products from peanuts. One product that we developed was "soy milk," which was given to patients at

157

SOUTH END

Henry Ford Hospital for experimental purposes. We made it in a huge, room-sized vat in the basement of the lab. It was like the soy milk that is sold everywhere today. The idea of soybean products that we use today was fostered from the soy research that we did back then. When I was hired, the big project was to create a sealant that would waterproof the cars, and I happened to develop the sealer that they used. Of course, I never got any credit for developing the process. From my work they were able to waterproof the cars so they could go through a car wash.

Ford was very aloof, and he would come through occasionally and bring visitors so he could show off what he was doing. Zasu Pitts, the famous silent film star, came through one time. We were not allowed to say anything to the visitors unless we were asked to do so. If not, we were not allowed to speak. I had to take down the experiment I was working on that day because they didn't want my work to draw the attention of the guests. We could not greet Mr. Ford unless he spoke to us first. I liked the research, but it was a hard place to work; it was hard not being valued as a person and contributor to the work being done.

After three years I decided that I wanted to return to teaching. I was the first African American science teacher at Northwestern High School in Detroit. They would only hire me to teach biology. Along with my teaching load, I also had to take care of the plants in the school — the personal plants of the other teachers in the building. There was a huge room at the back of my classroom with large windows for plenty of sunlight. The other teachers would bring their plants there for the winter, and I had to keep them alive. When the chemistry teacher retired, six years after I arrived, they moved me from biology to chemistry. I was the only one at the school who could teach chemistry. That meant that somebody else had to take care of the plants. Soon after that, I started the first science club at the school and became the sponsor of the school cheer team. I had never been a cheerleader myself. I always told my girls what to do, but I never demonstrated. I also expected them to be ladies. I loved teaching, working with the students and encouraging them to be the best people they could be. After I left teaching in the late 1980s, I began to realize that I had more of an impact on them than I ever realized while in the classroom.

I'm very proud of the fact that I'm still in touch with several of my students and they are still in touch with me.

WAITRESS IN THE SKY

Judi Gorsuch

"Mom, Dad, I've just been hired by TWA," I said.

"To do what?" they asked in unison.

"I'm going to be a stewardess," I replied.

"But what about teaching? You didn't graduate from college to become a waitress in the sky," huffed my mother.

"I'll only do it for a year or two until I've seen the world," I said.

I became a TWA stewardess (that's what we were called in the 1960s) almost by accident. I was a middle school teacher in 1966. When a colleague went to apply for a job with TWA, she invited me to join her. I went with her out of curiosity. Imagine my surprise when I was hired after a series of interviews, all based on appearances and poise. I'd always seen myself as ordinary-looking, certainly not the very pretty and poised stewardess I'd seen on my limited experience on commercial flights. Appearance was crucial as it added to the glamorous aspect of travel. Higher education wasn't necessary to become a stewardess, merely a course in charm school.

When I was hired by TWA, my parents were enraged, but their reaction fueled my determination to accept the job. I assuaged them by saying it would only be a year or two. I thought that would enough time to see the world. I planned to return to teaching, but that was not to be. After two years of European flying, I was hungry to see even more of the world. I was a stewardess for more than twenty years.

In the earliest years, the job was glamorous in large part due to the emphasis on outward appearance. Our designer uniforms were tailored with close-fitting jackets and slim skirts. We wore pancake-styled hats and snow-white gloves, and carried an extra pair of gloves and nylons.

The grooming regulations were stringent. No matter your shape, a girdle was required. Hair should not touch your collar and it had to show a visible curl. Makeup was specific: red nail polish and lipstick; eyeshadow, base, and mascara were mandatory. Weigh-ins were monthly. If you exceeded the maximum weight limit set by doctor's charts, you were put on the weight check. After an additional month of being over the weight limit, you were suspended from flying. After that you could be fired. Perfect appearance was an absolute must for stewardesses.

Because personal travel was the most important reason I continued to fly, I decided I was willing to accept the appearance regulations as a trade-off for the travel. And so the excitement of my job came from seeing new cities and new countries, and meeting new people. I would go to these places with the help of TWA's passes on other airlines. Even my parents were mollified when they used their first passes to Hawaii. That was the reason I started flying. I was able to see the Galapagos Islands, take an African safari, and travel by boat up the Nile. The stringent grooming and clothing requirements were a small price to pay considering the opportunity to see Madrid or Madagascar.

I think the desire to become a stewardess was buried in my brain earlier than I thought. My father took me up in a single-engine plane when I was eleven years old. The steep ascents and Dutch rolls absolutely thrilled me. I wanted more. It was only natural that I eventually chose a career of travel.

I read widely and dreamed of seeing faraway places depicted in books. I even attempted to live my dreams. For example, when I read *Heidi*, I begged my mother to obtain goat's milk and to serve it in bowls. When I read *Anne of Green Gables*, I pictured myself on Prince Edward Island.

When I was a junior in college, I accompanied a group of preadolescent girls from Michigan to Montana for a summer camp. It was my first commercial flight. The girls were amazed that I had never flown on a jet. "You mean you actually drove from Detroit to Denver, Colorado?" asked one of the girls. The Delta airline stewardesses on that flight impressed me. They handled their duties with grace and charm. I was envious. I wanted to be one of them.

From the beginning, I loved the environment in which I worked. Stepping into the interior of a plane was crossing a threshold of unique surroundings. The tasteful décor — rich burgundy and lush blue upholstered walls separating first class from coach — served as a reminder that all travelers were welcome and valued.

In the 1960s, there were a large number of first-time flyers. We assured them that flying was safer than driving a car, and we answered a myriad of questions. "How fast does the plane go? What time is it mid-Atlantic? How dangerous is turbulence? What should I see in London, Paris, or Rome?" Back then, passengers dressed differently for travel than they do today. Women wore dresses, often accessorized with hats and gloves. Men donned suits and ties or at the very least sports jackets. Even children were dressed in their Sunday best.

The galleys were neat and efficient; storage space and equipment were there to cater to passengers' dining needs. We kept drawers filled with decks of cards with pictures of different planes on them, children's games, and books. We even distributed junior pilot and stewardess wing-shaped pins, so that children would have mementos of their flight. Pilot wings for boys and stewardess wings for girls until the 1970s when men became flight attendants.

The dining services were designed for passenger comfort. First-class meals were elegant services with linen tablecloths and napkins, china, and crystal glassware. Tables were set individually, even including a fresh flower on each table. Meals were served in courses, beginning with caviar; a menu was presented to passengers depicting a choice for four entrées. Our service rivaled any top-notch

SOUTH END

restaurant. Even in coach, there was a choice of two entrées. Special meals were served to children; what kid doesn't like peanut butter and jelly? We could also accommodate vegetarians.

In addition to meal services, our primary duty was passenger safety. We spent most of our training time learning emergency procedures. Evacuations were handled with short, sharp commands: "Stand. Move. Jump." We didn't give passengers time to think about what they were doing.

During the late 1960s, TWA flew soldiers into Vietnam. These were called MATS (Military Air Transport) flights. We took very young men to war. They were enthusiastic and idealistic. We brought home boys who had turned into embittered, frightened men. These were confusing times for me. As an outspoken anti-war advocate, I didn't know if what I was doing was escalating the war. To this day, this remains the most poignant of my TWA memories.

The job changed drastically with the coming of the 747, the jumbo jet that tripled the number of passengers. The coach passengers were no longer offered a choice of entrées. Children's menus and toys were eliminated. The first-class service was no longer elegant. There were too many passengers to be able to interact with them personally. Prior to the 747's takeover of the skies, we were required to circulate throughout the cabin, initiating conservations about a passenger's destinations or commenting on his or her enthusiasm for flying.

When it finally came time for my wings to be clipped you'd think my wanderlust would have been sated. But that simply was not, nor will it ever be, the case. There are so many places I'd still like to see: Alaska, the Great Wall of China, the Great Barrier Reef, Nepal—all places I've never been. How thrilling it would be to experience any or all of them.

I was never simply a waitress in the sky. Instead, I was, and still am, a vagabond with an insatiable thirst for faraway places.

GIRL ENGINEER

Carol Blair

In 1969, after my freshman year of civil engineering courses at the University of Vermont, I wanted a summer job doing engineering work, but instead I was behind the counter at Al's French Fries. When I'd asked my advisor, Professor Milbank, about a summer job, he'd shrugged his shoulders. "The guys usually get field jobs with the highway department, but that's dirty work. I don't know," he said before walking away. I was stunned by this absurdity. *What does he mean, "dirty work"? I'm washable!* What I didn't understand then was that this man, approaching retirement, couldn't get his head around the idea that a woman could be an engineer.

After two weeks of making creamy cones, I got a brief interview with Fred Koerner, a civil engineer with his own business. He met my price — $1.75 an hour — and I had my start. I'd be helping four employees with surveys, concrete tests, and deed searches, making maps and copying plans. Mr. Koerner's office was by the Burlington Coca-Cola plant near Lake Champlain, five blocks down the hill from my parents' home. I rode my bicycle so I could be quick as

I collected and distributed plans around town. Except for the secretary, the office staff was all male. This was normal for me. From infancy when my parents put my crib in a bedroom with my two older brothers to my college classes with a hundred boys and men studying engineering, I'd always been surrounded.

That summer, I mastered a blueprint machine that collated plan sheets up to fifty inches wide and spewed the original back at me. I plucked each Mylar drawing from one table, laid it on a sheet of yellow blueprint paper from another table, and then lined it all up and fed it into the rollers. Then I'd catch the original and stack them on still another table.

Frequently stationed alone in that ammonia-filled room, I'd make as many as seventy-five copies of a set of two hundred sheets. I challenged myself to finish each set a little faster than the last, but my dedication and enthusiasm did not save me from boredom and weariness. Once, I closed my eyes, laid my head on my arms, and rested on the machine — right in front of the feeder rolls. Oh, how good it felt to stop. For a moment I drifted off, but then I felt my hair shift. *Wait! My hair! Oh, no!* I grabbed my braids and hit the reverse button. My hair was wound in both directions around the rollers. In a desperate tug-of-war with the machine, I won my ragged braids back and kept my scalp. The only evidence: a few hairs hanging from the rollers. It was many years before I told anyone. I hated to feed the idea that girls weren't suited for engineering work.

One day when the secretary was out, Mr. Koerner asked if I could type. "Not really," I said. He suggested that I "just try" and I sat down to type a deed search. I may have been at it for an hour or two, hunting and pecking, hardly making a dent in the project, when he found something else for me to do.

So, why was I so intent on being an engineer? Was it envy of my brother's Erector Set? As a kid, I was fascinated with the building of Interstate 89 through the Green Mountains. My parents often chose a highway construction site for road-trip picnics. We played on the huge tires of dump trucks and road graders and in the giant sandboxes created where they cut into the hills. I remember returning to one site for a lost flip-flop.

Construction was part of my daily life. My dad's do-it-yourself approach to our big Victorian home led to me helping him pour a foundation for our hundred-year-old carriage house when I was fourteen. So a career as an engineer didn't seem at all far-fetched.

My dad told me I should have a profession "in case I didn't get married." I didn't expect any man to want me, given my dad's admonishment that boys don't like tomboys, and my brother Ron's teasing, "Your cold nose is like a wet dog." (My parents kept heating bills low long before energy conservation was in vogue.) In retrospect, I can see I was primed for the gender struggle because I had nothing to lose. I hesitated only briefly at the thought that girls didn't *do* engineering. My brother was studying engineering and he was no smarter.

The next summer, I was an engineer's aide with the Vermont Highway Department. My crew worked on the Burlington Beltline (my family still calls this "Carol's Road"). We surveyed everything to ensure all was built according to plan and calculated quantities of

First day on the job, 1970

fill and concrete to reimburse the contractor. Our crew chief, Doug, kept us honest. We were delighted when he declared our work copasetic. Mert *("good 'nough fa' gov'munt wook")* was the elder and kept us entertained with his stories. Sometimes I set up the transit and took readings, but more often I was the "rodman" holding a human-size ruler vertically on the spot for which an elevation was needed, or suspending my plumb bob over a point to get its horizontal position.

The field office was a trailer that had just enough space for our crew. It contained an office for the site engineer, a tiny bathroom, space for a drafting table where plans could be lain out, a desk for calculations and paperwork, and storage for our equipment. The bathroom walls were so thin that every sound could be heard throughout the trailer, and I was very self-conscious.

One day, we were on a small roadwork project about fifty miles to the south, near no town. I had my period and anguished over my dilemma until the time came when I needed a bathroom (no towelettes in those days). I gathered my courage and walked to the nearest house, where I'd seen small children in the yard, hoping to use a restroom with privacy and running water. Thank God, there was a very understanding young woman there.

Another memorable day we inspected a new bridge over the railroad. To check the elevation every few feet along the length of each beam, Doug proposed we take turns, walking two beams each. I had never been afraid of heights, but this was not my grandfather's hay barn. A fall would land on the tracks thirty feet below. No harness. No net. When my turn came, I mounted the end of the beam, one foot ahead of the other between two rows of pegs that would anchor the rebar of the bridge deck. Mert handed me the rod. I rocked it back and forth slightly so Doug could get the reading. Then I stepped forward. As I lifted my boot, I felt it catch. The heads of those pegs felt like hooks. Heel to toe, my sweaty hands balancing the rod, I continued, one terrifying step at a time, all the way across, and then back on my second beam. I jumped down, quietly proud and *very* relieved.

For the summer of '71, I was promoted to Engineer's Aide II and worked in the planning office of the Vermont Highway Department in Montpelier. Trading jeans for a dress, I worked with six guys preparing plans for I-89. No more outdoor play; this was work. My tools were colored pencils, a big old ka-chunk-a-chunk calculator, and a planimeter—an ingenious mechanical device. When I traced the pointer around the perimeter of an irregular shape on a drawing, a series of wheels would roll and skid around the paper to measure the shape and calculate its area. I colored plans for public information meetings, calculated fill and stone for project estimates, and when it came my turn, dispensed coffee for everyone. Only the women took turns serving coffee. It's hard for me now to believe I didn't challenge this, but I thought I was lucky to be there and I wasn't about to rock the boat.

During my senior year, I worked on two engineering projects. One studied pedestrian crossings on the University of Vermont campus, and the other researched possibilities for the struggling local bus system. Both had real social impact. When I see the words "BUS STOP" on the back of bus stop signs in Burlington, I wonder why the recommendation I made as a college student became reality there, but in my forty years in Boston, it has not happened here.

Upon graduating, I married another engineering student, moved to Boston, and started my first full-time job as a junior engineer. But it would be years before I began to understand the persistent challenges of being a woman in my field.

IN THE DIRECTION
OF DREAMS

Kathryn M. Fairbanks

From an early age, I wanted just three things in life: to teach, to write, and to travel. I settled the first thing right off. In grade one, for first-grader reasons, I wanted to write on the blackboard, choose the monitors, and give out the paper. Born curious and enthusiastic, I wanted to know everything in the world as I suspected that teachers did. Dad's sister, Barbara Fairbanks Armstrong, taught in North Andover, and Ma's sister, Sister Catherine Bernadette, a Sister of Notre Dame, taught in Woburn, so my choice got the parental approval that firstborns often crave. No rebel was I, but I began noting things that I would do differently. I would never wear black health shoes with ugly Cuban heels; I wouldn't let another teacher criticize a child where he or the class could overhear; and I would never have flabby, flapping arms. (Two out of three isn't bad!)

By third grade, I wanted to write. The field of children's literature bloomed in the 1930s. Dr. Seuss's first book, *And to Think That I Saw*

It on Mulberry Street, published in 1937, was read to us in school. The Boston Public Library sent librarians out to sign students up for library cards right in class. Teachers got classroom book deposits from the BPL for us to read after we'd finished our work. All this gave us a familiarity with books, a love for reading, and an inspiration for writing.

Marion Sharp was my third grade teacher at the Mozart School on Beech Street in Roslindale. She was tall and had bright silver hair and large blue-grey eyes. Sometimes she wore a jacket made with lots of things that sparkled in fuchsia, silver, blue, and gold. I asked her what they were. "They're sequins," she said. I decided right then that when I became a teacher I'd always remember how much children notice what the teacher has on, and I'd wear lots of pretty clothes in my classroom. (When I became a teacher I always tried to do this.)

But I remember Miss Sharp best because she was the one who first told me I could write. For a shy child, it was a life-changing moment. I typed out a bunch of original verses, rhymed like those in *A Child's Garden of Verses* by Robert Louis Stevenson, one of the few books I owned at the time. I typed my poems on Dad's ancient Royal office typewriter, on tiny little memo paper because it was only kid stuff. Miss Sharp gave me a prize — a bunch of white typing paper. In our economical Yankee household, good white paper was used only for Dad's work and Ma's letters — until that day.

In seventh grade at the Robert Gould Shaw School, I heard that Marion Sharp had left the Boston Public Schools and entered the

Marist Order. She became Sister M. Susanna, and she was on the island of Tonga in the South Pacific. Four years later she died there.

In 1967, when my mother was buried in St. Joseph's Cemetery, West Roxbury, I saw a headstone a short distance away: SHARP. I looked closer. Miss Sharp's parents were interred there, but at the bottom of the stone a line had been added: *1902 Marion 1952 Sister M. Susanna, Marist in Wellington, New Zealand*. Then I remembered how she had once called me her "dear little poet." I cried.

Maybe I got the travel gene from Dad. He had sold maps door-to-door rather than work on the family farm in Vermont during the Great Depression. He loved maps and traveling all his life. He became a railway mail clerk for the U.S. Postal Service, working the mail on the trains from Boston to Montreal, to Bellows Falls or, in summer, to Hyannis. After he married Ma, had us kids, and bought a house in Roslindale, he managed to buy a small house trailer. By the end of our trailering vacation years, we had visited twenty-six states and four provinces of Canada. But it was Uncle Walter who helped me look even further.

We always knew that my uncle Walter Putnam was rich. He owned a Kodak 16mm movie camera and projector. He had a summer cottage on Cobbett's Pond in New Hampshire. And he subscribed to *National Geographic*. When we visited his family after one Christmas in the early forties when I was eight, he unexpectedly gave us a stack of his back issues. Overcome with the luxury of it all, we lugged them home in our '36 Ford and prepared to look upon life in other lands.

Kathryn at Abu Simbel

How clearly I remember some of those pictures. There were black and white photographs of New Guinea natives, warriors with terrifying, hideously beautiful markings incised or branded onto their bodies, patterns of swirling ropes or snakes or flowers, shining black skin carved like richly tooled leather. There was a series on American Indians with bright paintings by Langdon Kihn. I expected to see friendly Tonto types, but some of these pictures scared me about to death. Especially the witch doctor with his painted mask and rattle, whose curative intentions toward the patient I seriously doubted. There was a picture of a girl picking cherry-red coffee beans; I used that one in a geography project in fourth grade. There was another picture of a girl I didn't take to school. She was standing in a stream, smiling, combing back her long, wet hair, oblivious of the fact that she had nothing on above the waist. What she looked like naked, and the fact that she didn't care she was naked, were equally instructive.

But most thrilling to me was the 1941 *National Geographic* series, "Daily Life in Ancient Egypt" with Herget's classic paintings rendering into life dozens of Egyptian tomb carvings and cartoon-like drawings of Egyptians, at work, at war, at play. Each painting was captioned with the ancient text. The one I loved best was *"His Majesty went forth in a chariot of electrum, arrayed for war."* Decades later I saw that scene enacted in the film *The Ten Commandments* with a war-crowned Yul Brynner driving the chariot. And then there was the painting of a girl and boy playing in an Egyptian garden. Of course it was the rotten boy who got to have the dog, while the girl had to be content just tossing a ball. So, some things back then were the same as now!

The beauty of Egyptian art and architecture — temple columns topped with lotuses, princesses dipping water lilies from a Nile filled with fish and fowl — prompted me to beg Ma to take us to the Boston Museum of Fine Arts. They had a free day each week, our teacher said, and a magnificent Egyptian collection. Above glass cases filled with ancient Egyptian statuettes and vessels, I saw modern paintings of blue sky and golden sunlight on desert sand, pyramids and temples, and I knew that no matter how many years it would take me, I'd *have* to go there one day.

The route there was roundabout. In school, even near to Thanksgiving, we never heard much about Native Americans. Oh yes, we heard how they helped the Pilgrims, and then the teacher would start talking about painted Apache pots in Arizona. I wanted to know about our Massachusetts tribes. Where did they come from and when? And where are they now?

In the '70s I discovered a course called "Beneath Your Feet" at the Cambridge Center for Adult Education. It was about New England archaeology. I learned that before there were pyramids in Egypt, there were people living in the Blue Hills just south of Boston, practically next door to Mattapan and West Roxbury. And that at least some of them were ancestors of our Native Americans. For me, it was a stunning realization. It became an avocation that has become only more fascinating over the last forty years.

A bright, young Ph.D. archaeologist from Yale taught that course. I still tell Curt Hoffman that the smartest thing he did back then was to include membership in the Massachusetts Archaeological Society (MAS) in the course price. The local chapter held monthly meetings at the Trailside Museum in Milton. Saturdays he took us to visit sites being excavated not far away. I was hooked, and soon even helped out as chapter secretary.

One day I got a call from Marie Long in Mattapan. She'd been referred by Trailside. Would I look at what she thought was an Indian axe? Her late husband Frank, an oilman, had been converting a coal furnace to oil for a Milton homeowner. Frank felt inside it and knew that the old grate was propped up by a rock, which turned out to be a stone axe head. The owner said he'd found it when he dug up his garden, and it did the prop-up job just fine. The Society identified it as a full-grooved axe, made by Native Americans some five thousand years ago. Thanks to the Longs and Bill Taylor of MAS, it will become part of the MAS Museum's collection.

Kathryn, right, doing archaeology work at Beth Saida in Israel

After teaching for twenty years in the Boston Public Schools, you were entitled to a sabbatical year at half-pay, provided that you did twelve credits of college work. So I took the year, the half-pay, and did twenty-two credits at UMass Boston and field school at Clark University in Worcester. For the first time, I was studying for nothing but the love of learning. For two summers of weekends, I volunteered at the great Wapanucket site in Lakeville. It had twelve component sites, and C-14 dates going back nine thousand years. Massachusetts' first state archaeologist, Dr. Maurice Robbins, a founder of MAS, was there. At the lunch table he told us about all the archaeology going on in New England.

But totally unexpected life changes also resulted from that sabbatical year. The UMass chaplain at the time, Fr. Lennie Tighe of West

Roxbury, turned out to be an excellent Bible history teacher in a local parish, as well as a superb leader of pilgrimages to the Holy Land. At Capernaum on the Sea of Galilee, where Jesus lived for the three years of his ministry, I found that you could volunteer right there through the Biblical Archaeology Society of Washington, D.C. I worked for six weeks with the BAS team one summer, and then two other summers at Beth Saida nearby, the home of the fishermen apostles, Peter, Andrew, and Philip. Devout pilgrims to the Holy Land — Jewish, Christian, or Muslim — may tell you that being present at these holy places gives you a legacy for life. Forever after, when you read or hear your scriptures, the places, events, and people are familiar and dear to you. They become part of your life.

It was the connection with BAS that let me at last fulfill the childhood dream. They conducted tours to Egypt. We went for two weeks, ten days of it on the Nile aboard a Thomas Cook passenger vessel, *Serenade*. I found that the grandeur and beauty of Egypt was surpassed only by the good nature, musicality, and innate artistic sense you often could see in even the most ordinary Egyptians.

My teaching years now are good memories, the digging days are behind me, and the traveling shoes worn out. But by 1992, MAS had new headquarters in Middleborough, housing its Robbins Museum and a research library. They are totally maintained by volunteers. I'm happy to be one of them.

FROM BOSTON TO IRAN:
A PEACE CORPS EDUCATION

Patricia M. Walsh

Abbas, the *ambardar* (storekeeper), selected a key from his large rattling key ring, unlocked the door, and pushed it open to reveal a dusty, cobwebby room with books stacked high on shelves around the walls. Wasps, disturbed and annoyed, flew wildly in the sunlight that filtered through the dirty windows.

My assignment had been a big surprise. After three months of stateside training to be an English teacher, I arrived in Iran to learn that I was expected instead to organize a library in an agricultural college in the southwestern province of Khuzestan. I got my first library card when I was seven. I knew how to use the Dewey decimal system in the card catalog and was a frequent visitor to my local library, but I hadn't a clue how to organize one.

It was 1962. John Kennedy was president of the United States, and Reza Pahlavi was shah of Iran. At the time, the U.S. and Iran were on friendly terms. I was one of forty-three Peace Corps volunteers who would be the first group to be stationed in Iran, where we would

be split among thirteen agricultural high schools and colleges. My two-year assignment would be spent at Ahwaz Agricultural College (AAC). Five of us — two women and three men — would be working at AAC. The college was located about forty miles northwest of Ahwaz, the nearest town. The 1,240-acre campus sat on the east bank of the Karoon, Iran's major river, next to the large Arab village of Mollasani. Iranians are Indo-Europeans, not Arabs, but a large Arab population resides in the southwestern area of the country, on the border with Iraq.

Today, AAC is part of Shahid Chamran University in Ahwaz, but in 1962 it was in its infancy. Khuzestan is the oil-rich section of the country, and the National Iranian Oil Company (NIOC) had donated a large portion of land for the college. Former NIOC guesthouses and other buildings on the old part of the campus served as faculty and student housing, and as dining and storage rooms. Construction of new buildings — including classrooms, offices, and a library — was going on across campus, on the other side of a large date palm grove. Those rows of attached one-story concrete-block structures sat on a flat, dusty moonscape that was interrupted occasionally by irrigation ditches called "jubes." An oil pipeline ran along the road outside the campus.

While at the college, students were trained in agriculture and related fields for work in southwestern Iran's semi-arid conditions — a short rainy season, salty soil, and weather extremes. Summer temperatures in Khuzestan can soar to 140 degrees with little humidity, parching the soil. One faculty member told me, with a twinkle in his eye, that during very hot summers the local people would cool off by sitting in large clay jars filled with water up to their necks.

When the cache of books was moved to a temporary home on the new campus, I began making a list of them. The books' new home—a room that doubled as a classroom—was a problem in the making, and the object of a philosophical difference between the two co-directors who administered the college. Kentuckian George Luster, a Ph.D. in agriculture from Ohio State, wanted a circulating library. Jaffar Rassi, Cornell-trained in agricultural education and a former Ministry of Agriculture administrator and advisor, didn't approve of the idea; he believed that the students would not return the borrowed books. I thought it was worth a shot, particularly because the college of 150 students and 23 faculty members didn't have a bookstore nor any place to buy textbooks within hundreds of miles. Everything had to be ordered from Tehran or abroad.

The students were not familiar with a circulating library system so I had to explain it, student by student. Still, some of the books weren't being returned. What to do? How could I make the students understand how the new system would benefit them? Fines were an alien concept and too punitive, but because the library was composed mostly of single copies of books I couldn't allow them to, as Dr. Luster put it, "disappear." My roommate and I devised a plan for her to use materials from the American Library Association in her English classes, but still books weren't being returned.

In desperation, I decided to post the names of the offenders on the bulletin board located in the center of the campus. The bulletin board got lots of attention; the list got even more. I had created an uproar! In what seemed like seconds of its posting, the offenders raced across campus with the missing books, and begged

In the Ahwaz Agricultural College library with students

me take down the list. The list had the effect of the Boston Public Library posting the names of delinquent borrowers in the *Boston Globe:* shame. I never had to post another list. Still, I was sympathetic to the students. How were they to learn if one textbook had to be shared with all the other students in their class?

In February, seasonal torrential rains transformed the campus grounds into a shoe-sucking, boot-sucking swamp and poured through the roof of the temporary library, turning it into a wading pool. Miraculously, the books were spared, and eventually the library moved into its own space.

Meanwhile, without the aid of a computer, the Internet, or Google, I was tackling the ongoing task of cataloging the collection of 1,700 books on topics such as agronomy, poultry diseases, animal science, plant diseases, agricultural mechanics, horticulture, and entomology. Some of the books were in Persian, French, or German, but they were all undecipherable to this Boston-born novice whose knowledge of agriculture was limited to my father's backyard garden. But I learned fast. I enlisted faculty members to help me sort out the collection, and provide me with lists of additional books to order. My vocabulary was expanding rapidly: salt-tolerant crops; avian leukosis complex; water table; ecology; soybeans; land management; soil erosion — wow, was I a long way from home. My dad would have loved it there.

During the summer of 1963, when the college was closed, I received library science training in two libraries in Tehran, the Abraham Lincoln Library and the University of Tehran's Institute of Parasitology and Tropical Medicine. That summer was also the time of major riots across the country after the shah arrested religious leader and political activist Ayatollah Ruhollah Khomeini for speaking out against the shah's westernizing policies and for threatening his regime. The Iranian government imposed curfews on Iranians and foreigners alike. It was a very uncertain time.

The best part of my job was the students. Although I have forgotten the names of many of them, I do remember thinking how much easier *my* education had been. I remember their interest in learning English and their formality, especially Mr. Boland's. That wasn't his real name, but I called him that because he was so tall. (The word for "tall" in Persian is *boland*.) Mr. Boland would open the library door, bow his head slightly, place his hand over his heart and, in his best archaic English, say, "I am your thrall." Often, as he passed by the windows that ran across the upper half of the library's walls, he would mouth the same words. A total charmer. Years later I would learn that he had died in an auto accident. Another student had a passion for soybeans. He would stand in front of my desk extolling at length the virtues and possible uses of a legume I had never seen. He was way ahead of his time. Once I agreed to let a student display his paintings in the library. His art—that he said depicted the misery of mankind—featured manacled arms reaching up from churning seas toward dark menacing clouds, and was a source of amusement for his fellow students. I often wondered why he was studying agriculture.

When President Kennedy was assassinated it was nighttime in Iran so it wasn't until eight o'clock the next morning when two students came to Dr. Luster's home, where my roommate and I were visiting, with the terrible news and their condolences. We were stunned and disbelieving until Dr. Luster turned on the radio to Voice of America and we heard the words that broke our hearts: "President Kennedy is dead."

That day, three students came by the library to borrow some *Time* magazines. I learned why a few hours later as the American volunteers and staff—including Dr. Luster and his wife; the American animal husbandry instructor, his wife, and three children; and two other volunteers from Ahwaz—walked up the stairs to the student dining room where a memorial service had been arranged in our

Patricia Walsh at the Ahwaz Agricultural College

honor. Taped to a dining room window were two small handwritten posters—one in English and the other in Persian—each with a photo of John Kennedy. Inside, Dr. Rassi stood behind a small table with a single vase of flowers and told the grieving Americans, "Remember that he belonged not only to you. He belonged to us, as well." It was a simple and touching tribute to the man who had inspired me and so many others to join the Peace Corps.

A few days later our friend, Jimmy Obayat, died trying to rescue a worker on the crew that was bringing electricity to our campus. We had visited his village on the Iraqi border a few months before and he introduced us to his unique Marsh Arab community built entirely on water. Jimmy had been planning to study in the States.

That November was the lowest point in my two years in Iran.

A few months later, in February 1964, our students went on strike. That year, the college was scheduled to graduate its first four-year class, but because the Ministry of Education had not decided what degree the students would receive, the students refused to attend classes until their demand—that they receive the same degree as graduates of other agricultural colleges in Iran—was met. They threatened to go en masse by train to Tehran to make their case in person to the ministry.

The campus was very tense. The administration and faculty were furious. An emergency staff meeting held in the library was very strained. Usually talkative faculty members were subdued. We had all heard the rumors. Agents of SAVAK, the shah's notorious secret police, were suspected of being among the students. Were they instigating the strike? Were they a threat to the strike leaders? Were the students in danger? No one mentioned any of that during that meeting. The shah had "eyes and ears" everywhere. Dr. Luster learned this first-hand during a meeting with some Iranian officials in town. Their request: "Tell us the names of the strike leaders, and we will 'take care of them.'" Dr. Luster was stunned. As upset as all of us were with the students' actions, it was unthinkable that we would turn over any of them to persons we suspected of being SAVAK agents.

Eventually things got back to normal. Screens were added to the library windows to keep Mollasani's insect-rich world from flying in at night and covering the ceiling lights or biting everyone in sight. Students received library cards, and some worked part-time in the library. The book collection was expanded. More shelves and furniture were added. Faculty members shared library duty at night. A clean water system and a dependable electricity system greatly enhanced the quality of life on campus. The college continued experiments growing salt-tolerant crops, but also launched a United Nations project to drain salt from the soil.

Shortly after my return to the States, my father and I met a neighbor in the local supermarket. My father proudly introduced me as his daughter who had just returned from the Peace Corps. "That's nice," the neighbor replied, then turned and continued on with her shopping. My father and I were taken aback by her lack of interest.

But what if she had asked, "What was it like? What did you learn?" Today, I would tell her how exciting it was to live in a country with such an ancient past, that Iranian food is delicious and Iranian hospitality is legendary, that Iranians — like the Irish — love poetry, that traditional Iranian architecture is magical, that entering a Persian carpet shop is a test of will power, and that Iranian merchants love to bargain. The many Iranians who taught me about their history, politics, geography, humor, art, literature, and, of course, agriculture, also changed my view of the world and of my own country. It's no wonder that fifty years later my fond memories of Iran remain tucked in a corner of my heart.

Moving Up and Moving On

A STORY OF SURVIVAL

Leo Gillis

I am lucky I survived childhood. I was almost killed three different times. The first time I don't remember, because I was two years old. I was playing on my father's truck, but he didn't know I was there, and he started to drive away. I fell off and broke my collarbone and was almost run over by the rear tire. I was born in the Savin Hill section of Dorchester. Later we moved to Bispham Street, which was probably the last dirt road in Boston, in an area of Dorchester called Fields Corner. On our first day there, I took a walk on Park Street and walked all the way up to the Park Theater and could not remember which way I came from. I walked up Dorchester Avenue to Gibson Street, and down Gibson to Bispham and found my home again. In the old neighborhood, the police would find me and buy me ice cream whenever I got lost. But not in Fields Corner.

The second time I nearly died, I fell of the roof of a building still under construction. I fell three floors to the ground. The third time, I was on the back of a trolley car at the corner of Dorchester Avenue and Gibson Street. In those days, we liked to hitch a ride on the back of the trolley rather than pay. It usually worked with no problems because the driver couldn't see us. That time when I grabbed the trolley, the ground wire came loose. A ball of electricity came down and hit me on my head. I was knocked unconscious, and taken to Boston City Hospital. This one made the newspapers.

When we were young, we did not have a TV. Mrs. Cadigan on the third floor had a TV and we would go upstairs to watch hers. My father would make Mrs. Cadigan a large cup of coffee and we got to watch the *Mickey Mouse Club*, which was the only show we watched in those days.

When I was in the Rochambeau School in Dorchester, I never took my lunch on Fridays. Money did not go far enough in those days, so my brothers and sisters and I would go to school without lunches at the end of most every week. My mother worked nights cleaning offices and later on she worked in a laundry. When she got paid on Fridays, she would rush to the store to buy food for our lunches and bring it to school. But there were many weeks in elementary school when we had no lunch on Friday. This caused me some embarrassment and anger especially when our teacher would ask the other kids in class to share their lunches with me. I came to hate school for that reason. I remember taking a test and I passed and was above the national average, but I started to skip school. This continued throughout my school years until I quit school at the age of sixteen.

As a teenager I had personal problems in my life, and I turned to alcohol. My father would not tolerate drinking in his house. He was a former drinker himself. He stopped drinking when my mother was pregnant with me. It was New Year's Eve, the last night of 1938, and a major storm took the roof right off the house. He quit with my godfather. They made a pact not to drink again after they woke up the next morning and found that there was no food in the house. That's why they decided to stop drinking. Only my father stuck with it.

In my teens, when my father would throw me out of the house, I would sleep anywhere. In warm weather, I slept in parks. In cold weather, I went to a heated waiting room in Fields Corner station. I did not have a problem with that and my drinking progressed. I could not hold on to jobs and that was also a problem.

My life was bad for several years, lasting through my twenties until I got into recovery. One morning, I started drinking early with two friends and we barhopped up Dorchester Avenue. The last bar we stopped at we were drunk and looking for trouble and we found it. I had just met one of the guys I was drinking with the night before, and that morning he started a fight with another man. My new friend punched the other man and knocked him off the barstool. The man pulled out a gun and hit my friend in the face. I tried to stop him, and he stuck the gun in my stomach and told me to get back on the stool, which I did. The bartender was a friend of the man with the gun, and also had a gun and he hit me across my head with his gun. That's when I grabbed my friend and ran out of the bar. We were taken to Boston City Hospital and we both got stitches on our faces. Both men in the bar were caught and served time in prison. I never saw the man I was drinking with or the other men again.

My oldest brother had stopped drinking by then, and he would try to help me, but I would not stop. He got my cousin George to stop drinking. I had known George most of my life. He would come to my house a lot when we lived on Bispham Street in Fields Corner, then on Adams Street across from Ronan Park. I drank with George a few times through the years, but not very often. My drinking got worse as I grew older.

My brother took me to an AA meeting and George started talking to me and would ask me to go to a meeting with him. I would always refuse until the last time I said yes, and that changed my life. Almost immediately I got a job and stayed with it for several months. I have put that drinking life behind me for the past forty-one years.

When I first got sober I needed to make many changes in my life, which I did in part by being able to hold on to jobs. I also needed to make changes in me. For example, it was hard to talk to people, something I have never fully gotten over, even today. But I am doing better by pushing myself to make new friends. I also got married and now have four daughters and three grandchildren, two boys and one girl.

In my first years of sobriety, I had several jobs until I started working with the City of Boston taking 9-1-1 calls. I retired from this job in 2002 after twenty-three years there. That job was good for me. I know I made some mistakes but I also know I helped people who were in trouble and that helped me appreciate what I had. One time I took a call from a woman who was hiding in her bathroom. Someone had broken into her house and was still in the house, and I stayed on the line with her, keeping her calm until the police arrived.

At first my retirement was difficult for me. I had no income for several months and I could not find another job for a while. I lived with my oldest daughter Jennifer until I found a job delivering food for a local restaurant, which helped me financially and gave me something to do. I worked there for about eighteen months. Then I got a job at Logan Airport. I worked there for about three years. I no longer work because I have arthritis in both knees. I would still work if I could, but I do have another life and newfound friends and things I can do. And my family keeps me busy. Sometimes my grandkids will come to stay. I like where I live now in my neighborhood. I still think of each day as a blessing.

SUN FROM ANOTHER GARDEN: MY JOURNEY FROM GEORGIA TO BOSTON AND BEYOND

Dorothy Perryman

I remember standing perfectly still in the secret place that I visited daily. It was the perfect place for reflection and refuge, wedged among endless rows of green and yellow corn stalks that stood tall and straight like soldiers. I loved going there to invoke my magic of making time stand still by my sheer will. Standing there peering up into the sky was like being at the movies. Shades of vivid blue was the background canvas for white cotton-candy clouds that were so animated they appeared to morph into a parade of animals, angel wings, or faces that stared back at me. Golden rays of sunshine beamed hotly down upon me, enveloping me like a garment. I pretended it made me invisible to everyone but God. While munching on a sweet juicy stalk of sugar cane, I would share my secrets and ask Him questions that any five-year-old would ask.

That day, my questions centered on why my family and I had to leave this beloved place. We grew potatoes, watermelons, green vegetables, tomatoes, beans, and peanuts. We had many nut- and fruit-bearing trees, such as walnuts, pecans, figs, apples, pears, and muscadine grape vines. I could not imagine leaving behind our cows, pigs, chickens, horses, and our black hound named Prince. I told God how sad and angry I was when my father first told my sister Barbara and me that the family would be leaving the farm to move up north for better opportunities and better schools. Even though I did not fully understand what my father meant, I did understand that one day soon would be my last in this place that had become sacred to me. It was like being in the Garden of Eden and I had no choice but to give it all up. God did not give me answers to my many questions; however, I did feel better just talking about it.

Having overheard bits and pieces of my parents' conversations about taking a vacation to Boston to visit our aunts, uncles, and cousins, I began to understand why my uncles and their families had made so many trips to Boston prior to moving there. They had their own trucks to transport furnishings and belongings and eventually secured housing and employment, and enrolled their children in school. The plan was that we would visit for two weeks during the summer of 1948 and return to Georgia. Six to eight months later, our belongings would be driven to Boston by our uncles and we would take the train. We would live with my aunt and uncle in their apartment until my parents found jobs. After that we would move into a place of our own and get enrolled in school.

When summer came, we drove to Boston to visit. Although I was happy to see our cousins who used to live on a farm not far from us,

I hated that Boston was mostly concrete and bricks everywhere except for a few trees lining the cobblestone streets and sparse patches of grass dotted here and there. It seemed silly to me that people lived in uniform rows of three- and four-story red brick buildings stacked upon one another. The skies were often cloudy, dark, and dreary. Many days were cold and damp. I missed my daily dose of Georgia sunshine that covered me like a warm blanket. Never could I imagine coming back here to live.

My father instructed us on appropriate social behaviors, rules, and regulations according to the environment. He did not want us exposed to the divisive, negative environments of social separation between the races. My sister Barbara had attended a segregated school for a short period of time but I was too young, thereby escaping the brunt of whites-only signs and separate facilities. Living on the farm had provided a sheltered environment for me that was free from the impact of direct racism. The closer the time came to leave, the sadder I felt. However, the majority of our extended family had already settled in Boston. Left behind were elderly aunts and uncles who had decided to remain in Georgia.

Seven months later in the winter of 1949, the train ride to Boston was the most thrilling nighttime adventure. I saw standing on the tracks a long, black iron dragon with many doors, windows, and seats. The smoky night air was the only residue in the calm star-filled sky. My heart was pounding and I could hear it echo in my ears. We girls clutched our father's huge hands for dear life. We began to giggle and make fun of this humongous metal contraption that would carry us from the countryside into the city. We were hoisted up one by one into the black metal tube that began huffing and puffing as the conductor began chanting, "All aboard! All aboard!" Once we were seated, the conductor called, "Tickets, please! Tickets, please!" My eyes were able to focus upon the dim light in the car, which was filled with many faces of strangers who stared back at me. We were excited, exhausted, hungry, and delighted that our mother had prepared a fried chicken supper box for all of us. I remember falling asleep while promising myself that someday I would return to Georgia.

Upon arrival in Boston, our family of five moved in with a family of six — our aunt, uncle, and four of our cousins — in their small apartment in a brownstone in the South End. My father obtained a job at a mattress factory within a couple of months and my mother became employed a month later as a seamstress in a factory making women's undergarments.

Several months later we were able to move into our own three-bedroom apartment in another three-story red brick brownstone next door. We were not allowed to go outside the apartment when our parents were at work because they were unfamiliar with our neighbors and the businesses in the neighborhood. Eventually we were allowed to go out on the steps and our cousins helped introduce us to the neighborhood children, candy stores, and local businesses. Our neighborhood was a melting pot of ethnic, cultural, and racial diversity with a multitude of languages and ethnic dress. Immigrant families consisting of second and third generations lived harmoniously together. Delicious aromas would float from kitchen windows and restaurants in every direction. It was common practice to ask people, "Where are you from?" or to ask about their culture and

Freddie Paul Perryman and his daughters, Barbara and Dorothy

language. I discovered our neighbors were Greek, German, Italian, Hispanic, Asian, Jewish, and Portuguese. Local merchants often gave a line of credit to neighbors in-between their paydays. We were allowed to make purchases on a neighbor's behalf. Accounts were always settled at the end of the week on payday.

Prior to enrolling us in school, my father once again explained to us that we moved up north to get good jobs and better educational opportunities for us. My mother and father had only an elementary school education because they had to work the farm. His ultimate goal for us was to get a high school diploma.

He also informed us that although there were no whites-only signs or other segregated signs in public, we might still experience some type of discrimination because of the color of our skin. We were further instructed in classroom etiquette by addressing the teacher respectfully by their last name. We had to raise our hand to ask or answer a question. In the event we had to use the restroom, we had permission to leave the room if we were being ignored. If the teacher had a problem with that we were to tell the teacher to contact our father and he would handle it. If other kids did not want to play with us, we were not to worry about it. We were to do our very best at all times and the only A's that were required were in "Conduct" and "Effort."

In September of 1949, my mother enrolled us girls in John J. Williams Elementary School. It was in the first grade that I was formally introduced to books. Learning to write and read became an exciting adventure. I became an avid reader and developed a passion for books, which became a doorway leading into worlds of knowledge and wonder. My mother also took us to the public library so that we could check out books for extra reading.

The school population reflected the neighborhood populations. Many of the kids in class were the neighborhood kids that we already played with at home. Our class picture looked like the United Nations. I received a multicultural educational experience that I will never forget. Many of these friendships lasted throughout high school.

One of my favorite subjects in school was history and it was then that I discovered my family and myself in the history books. We were participants in what was called the Great Migration, which occurred between 1915 and 1960 when World War I created tremendous demand for workers in the factories up north as men went off to war. Between World War I and the presidency of Richard Nixon, around six million blacks made an exodus from the racial oppression they endured in the south and headed north or west to escape lynching, an unjust legal system, social and educational inequality, inequality of employment, and denial of voting rights.

My parents were sharecroppers in Madison, Georgia. This was still considered a plantation-like economy and most blacks were sharecroppers, tenant farmers, or farm laborers. This prompted me to question my parents about the farm I loved so much. They informed me that it never was our family farm. A white gentleman owned the house and land. He paid my parents a few dollars and allowed them to farm the land for food.

In the spring of 1982 I fulfilled my dream of returning to Georgia. I relocated to Atlanta and lived there for four years. It was wonderful to reconnect with my southern roots.

The more I learned the more grateful I was to my father for his vision for our family. He did indeed empower us to obtain a higher level of prosperity. All of us girls, Barbara and I and our younger sister Betty, graduated from high school and we all went on to obtain college degrees in various disciplines. My father eventually became a carpenter and construction worker and he and his brothers helped to build many of Boston's medical facilities and other buildings throughout the city. Although he has passed away, his legacy to us and to this city still lives on.

SOUTH END

LEAVING HOME

Ita Bridges

Although Ireland, my native country, was not involved in World War II, I did feel the tension and uneasiness in daily life during my teenage years. There was rationing and shortages of goods that seemed to last forever. It was also hard to find work. My older sisters Phil and Eva had left our town of Roscommon and gone to England to train as nurses, and my two brothers Gerry and Paddy had also gone to England to work. There was no work for me after I graduated from high school. So, I decided to go to England, too, and train to be a nurse. I was accepted to St. James Hospital in Balham, London, where my sister Eva was in her final year of training. It felt good to have a goal in life, even though the workload was heavy and the pay small.

My cousin, Nancy, lived in Boston and we had corresponded as pre-teenagers. She was an only child, where I was the fifth of ten children. Both of us enjoyed hearing about events outside of our worlds, and sharing our ideas and dreams. When Nancy became engaged to Eddie, a Boston policeman, she wrote to me and asked me to be her maid of honor. My heart was aflutter. It was a big decision to make as I was in the middle of my training, but then the lure of going to America was pulling me in that direction. I really could not afford to take a trip to the U.S. for any reason at age twenty-one, so I wondered if I should emigrate. I discussed everything with my sister and parents and then decided. I was young, with my whole life before me, and I could always go into nursing in America. My aunt paid my passage to Boston, with a promise that I would repay her when I got a job.

My first job in the U.S. was at Keystone Factory, which lasted four months. I was laid off before Christmas. Then I got a job in the Waldorf cafeteria in City Square as a waitress. I wasn't crazy about that job, as nursing was my goal. I had applied to Boston City Hospital to restart my nursing training, but I wasn't accepted because I didn't have enough science in my résumé and was advised to take some courses in a preparatory school and reapply. Alas, I didn't have any money to pay the tuition. Then I was able to get a job at Children's Hospital in Boston as a nurse's aide. I was happy there and my former training helped me to adjust quickly to the hospital routine. My work schedule was 7:00 AM to 3:00 PM one week, and then 3:00 PM to 11:00 PM the next week.

Five weeks after I arrived in Boston, Eddie arranged for his friend Doug to come with him to meet me. They called me "the Irish colleen." So the four of us went out to dinner at Wollaston Beach and to me it was a wonderful time. Doug was stationed at the Fargo Building in South Boston. He was a second class petty officer in the U.S. Navy, attached to the supply department.

Doug called me the next day and asked me if I would like to go to the movies. I said yes, and before I knew it we were seeing each other on a daily basis. When I worked the 3:00 to 11:00 shift, he would pick me up at 11:00 PM and travel with me on the subway to Fields Corner and then take the bus with me to Westglow Street in Dorchester. He would walk me to my house, and give me a quick kiss before he had to rush back to the corner to pick up the last bus back to Fields Corner. The bus driver would stop at the head of the street and wait for him.

Doug showed me the sights of Boston, took me on the Freedom Trail, to see the USS *Constitution*, the waterfront, the Public Garden, and to my first ice hockey game, which fascinated me. He was always kind, generous, and considerate, and we enjoyed each other's company.

Nancy and Eddie were married on June 11, 1949. Doug had been transferred to the USS *Salem*, a heavy cruiser, which was in the process of being equipped for commissioning. Before that ship sailed on its maiden voyage, Doug and I became engaged and decided to marry in a year or so. It was hard being separated while he was at sea, but I had a wedding to plan. Doug's parents were very helpful and everything went okay. We were married on October 21, 1950. Unfortunately none of my family could come to our wedding. The trip would have been far too expensive. Even transatlantic calls were rare and expensive in those days, but Doug had arranged to have me phone home the day before our wedding so I could I talk with my whole family.

In July 1951, while Doug was in the Mediterranean, he was offered a transfer to the admiral's staff. He asked me if I would come to France to live for two years as part of the deal, and I jumped at the chance. I left by boat that December, and Doug met me in Naples, Italy. We traveled by train to France, where we had a place to live in the quaint village of Villefranche-sur-Mer, which was only five miles outside of Nice.

Although I had taken French in school, it wasn't the same listening to the spoken language, but I soon picked up the patois of the natives and somehow managed to understand and make myself understood. When buying groceries, I could identify canned goods by their labels and as fresh fruits and vegetables were plentiful, I had no trouble there. In the beginning I had to point to whatever I needed. I did my shopping daily as I didn't have a refrigerator.

Two years quickly became seven years and during that time I had four children. The navy community was mostly young brides at that time, so the pregnancy rate grew and I helped other new mothers with doctor's visits. We formed a navy wives club and would meet once a week to discuss problems we were having. Sometimes we needed to collect baby clothes for newborns along with cribs and strollers until the ship came in. Most wives ordered their baby layettes from the states, which were delivered via FPO on the ship.

In 1958, Doug was transferred to London. It was sad leaving the friends I'd met in France and the laid-back life I'd come to enjoy. What I loved was having my husband home every night. Doug could take the bus into work in London, and shopping for me was a bus ride away. Fortunately, a horse-drawn wagon came by once a week and stopped at our door so I could buy cereal, bread, eggs, and canned goods. We had our fifth child in England, shortly before Doug was transferred back to Boston.

In 1961, we moved to Brighton where we expected to stay for a long time. We had convenient access to downtown Boston on the subway. We enjoyed walking in the Public Garden and on the Freedom Trail. There was a supervised playground on the Boston Common where I could leave my children in safety to play while I went shopping in Filene's at Downtown Crossing.

One of my daughters, Michele, liked to go sailing on the Charles River. She took lessons at Charles Street. There was a bowling alley on Soldiers Field Road within walking distance of us, which my family enjoyed. There was also a swimming pool and skating rink nearby. The city was beautiful at Christmastime and we especially enjoyed the lighting of the Christmas tree. Another attraction was the Easter Parade on Commonwealth Avenue, also the Boston Pops orchestra playing on the Esplanade on the Fourth of July. As a navy family, we enjoyed visiting the USS *Constitution* at the Charlestown Navy Yard.

There are four seasons in New England, each with its own beauty and activities, and I feel blessed to be part of this community.

Looking back, I was pretty flexible and easily adjusted to living and rearing a beautiful family in three different countries. My beloved, wonderful husband, Doug, passed away on February 27, 2007, and I still miss him very much, but the children are all close to me. Military life can keep families together even when they are living apart. I will always be proud to have been a navy wife.

Change is inevitable — except from a vending machine.
ROBERT C. GALLAGHER

CHANGES

Ilene Katz

I hate change and like routine. For fifty-four years, I lived in the same apartment building, 2212 Plumb First Street, Apartment 4E, Marine Park, Brooklyn, New York, 11229 — a crooked area off Canarsie waters and the Rockaway harbor. The building was constructed of reddish brown stone with glass windows out front. It was six stories high and had eight apartments on each floor. There was nothing exceptional about the building except that it was a co-op. You owned your unit and received shares for it. Over time the share prices increased, which made the apartments more valuable, especially in a city like New York.

My parents purchased our unit in 1952 for $890. Initially five of us crammed into its four rooms — my parents, my maternal grandmother, my brother Mark, and me. Marine Park was your typical working-class Jewish neighborhood. It was full of small family-owned businesses. Across from our building was the commercial district — a triangular block lined with a candy store, beauty parlor, grocery store, butcher, and bakery. If you needed anything, it was in the neighborhood.

My mother was a beautician who worked long days in the beauty parlor. From Thursday to Saturday, she'd work forty hours. As a child, I would run small errands for the women in the shop and their customers, getting coffee or soda from the candy store. They'd give me a two-cent tip. In those days, that was the most change I'd known. Everything in my childhood world had a blissful routine and I liked it that way.

It was when I got to high school that real changes began to affect my life. I'd been studious up to then, even skipping one grade, but I fell in with a new set of partying friends and began socializing. I guess I wanted a change from being the kid who was mostly alone. By the tenth grade, I'd flunked three classes and dropped from an above-average student to one who was barely making it. My father warned me that the kids I was hanging out with were not at my level, but I didn't listen. Change was starting to knock on my door.

After high school, I went to City College to study business. Following graduation, I began a career in retail. I worked for a few retailers in Brooklyn before working my way up to an assistant buyer for the corporate offices of MH Fishman and Lamston in Manhattan. Day in and day out, year in and year out, I took the bus and train, back and forth, into the city for fifteen years until both companies went bankrupt. My routine consisted of going to work, coming home, making dinner, washing dishes, watching TV, and preparing for the next day.

I'd always liked things uniform, even my dress. Each day, I wore a men's tailored oxford shirt over bell-bottomed polyester slacks with a matching blazer. I had oxford shirts in all colors of the rainbow—pink, lilac, baby blue, pale yellow, and of course the standard white. I liked to think I was dressing for business but I was really just expressing myself, who I am: serious.

After my father died when I was twenty-one, I continued to live in the apartment with my mother until her passing in 1988. During those seventeen years of living with mother, I'd thought about moving out but the cost of living and fear of the unknown held me there. I knew everyone in the old neighborhood, plus I was invested in it; I didn't want to lose out on my shares. With her passing came drastic changes in my life and my routine. For the next fifteen years, I lived alone, did a little traveling (California, Oklahoma, and Kentucky), but was mostly unemployed because I couldn't catch on to the computers that had taken over the retail industry. After awhile, I lost my way and stopped caring for myself; eventually I got very ill. My sickness meant that I would have to depend on my brother and sister-in-law for help, which brought about the biggest change in my life so far—coming to Boston to live.

I came to be near them so they could help with my care, and I have had to adjust to a whole new way of life. I haven't decided if the changes are good or bad. The worst parts have been leaving behind fifty-four years of memories: the borough of Brooklyn, five hundred books, dozens of my favorite oxford shirts, cat statues that mother and I collected because they reflected our name (Katz), a vase I bought in Mexico that broke while I was packing, pictures,

217

WEST ROXBURY

needlepoints… the list goes on and on. Initially, I was placed in assisted living, going from four rooms to one. However, because of the cost, I eventually had to get my own place. I now live in West Roxbury where I have a spacious apartment with large rooms and a back porch. There are trees, features that we rarely had in New York. I have so much room now in comparison to Brooklyn, that I can get exercise just by walking through my house. The area is peaceful, but I'm still uncomfortable and haven't made enough friends. I haven't become a Bostonian yet, and I never will. I'm going to keep my New York accent. It's a little hard to change that after fifty-four years.

LIFE IS GOOD

Dolores Seay

Bernard was the fourth child and the second boy in my family. He was the toughest of my three brothers. You could tell that John Wayne was his favorite movie star just by the way he carried himself. He had a John Wayne–type walk and a no-nonsense demeanor. As a young man, he liked the ladies and thought he was a great dancer. Bernard never married and never had children, although he loved kids and they loved Uncle Bernie. He was a painter and loved his job, but he drank alcohol — a lot of alcohol — and he developed liver cancer. He had successful liver resection in 2009, but the cancer came back in 2012.

I found out that he was sick and took him to the hospital where he was admitted for tests and a biopsy. The results showed that the cancer was beyond treatment. Rather than move into a nursing home, he asked if he could come to my house. I said yes and made arrangements with hospice to have a bed and everything he needed to be delivered to my house the next day. My sister Diane and I were told that he would live for weeks or months. He was brought to my house by ambulance the next day, a Friday. He was able to get off

the gurney and walk up the nine steps to my house. He didn't want to get in bed. He wanted to sit in the living room and watch TV, so I let him. He ate very little, almost nothing, but the hospice nurse said not to worry about it.

The people from the hospice agency were wonderful to us. They didn't mind my calls and answered all my questions. The nurse came whenever I needed her, outside of her daily visit. The family and all the kids came to my house Friday night and, as sick as he was, he seemed glad to see everyone. Friday night he was okay. Saturday afternoon he was okay. That evening he complained of pain and I called hospice. They advised me over the phone to break out the emergency kit they had sent and what and how to administer the medication, which I did, and by the time the nurse arrived, he was feeling better.

Sunday morning he woke up really agitated and I could hear a kind of wheezing when he breathed. I tried to calm him down by talking and rubbing his back. He seemed like he didn't know what to do with himself. He would lie down and then jump up to a sitting position. Then he'd jump to his feet but couldn't move his feet to take a step. I called hospice and they said someone would be on their way. Then he acted like he couldn't catch his breath, but I thought it was more like being overwhelmed. My daughter and granddaughter arrived before the nurse and we tried to get him comfortable in bed. The nurse came and administered meds and he calmed right down. The nurse called us outside the room and told us that he was actually dying. She said it might be tonight, maybe tomorrow. There was no way of knowing. We went back into the room. My granddaughter prayed. I held his hand and said a prayer and told him, "If you have to go, Bernard, it's okay. I'll see you in the Resurrection." He stopped breathing. I called to the nurse who pronounced him dead. It happened so quickly.

In the weeks after Bernard's death, I thought a lot about our childhood. We were born in lower Roxbury in the 1940s. We lived on Washington Street and our second floor apartment was level with the el. We could look in the window of trains passing by and we kids would guess where people were going and pretend that they saw us.

We lived in what I guess was a cold-water flat, because I remember every morning my mother had big pots of water boiling on the stove to wash with. We had a bathroom with a tub, but it was in the hall and my mother never let us bathe in it. We took a bath in the kitchen in a galvanized tub. My mother would say, "Now hurry up before the water gets cold." The next one had to use the same water. If my father was home when we bathed, he would check our ears and noses and clean them with a hair pin if necessary.

The toilet in the bathroom had a pull chain and made a loud sound when pulled. It always reminded me of a train and the driver pulling the train horn. It was freezing in that bathroom and there were no windows. We had only one bedroom. My parents slept in there and we kids had a pullout couch and cots.

Every year just before Christmas, my mother took us to Mechanics Hall where a big Christmas party was held every year for kids. It was probably sponsored by the city or the mayor's office. I don't even remember where that was located, but I looked forward to going there. I was around five or six years old. I don't remember if there was a show or something, but I remember a stage. Every family left with a shopping bag or bags. I think I remember us getting winter coats and boots. But I most certainly remember the fruit basket with the Christmas apples. They were delicious and I loved them. I only remember seeing them in that bag from Mechanics Hall at Christmastime and I couldn't wait to eat one.

My parents stayed together fifty-five years and had seven children. My mother was the disciplinarian of the two and she was only four foot eleven. There were four girls (Dolores, Diane, Denise, and Darlene) and three boys (Bobbie, Bernard, and Bruce). I am the oldest. My mother never had many friends and she was always at home. A few times she sat outside with a few of the neighbor ladies, but one day as they were sitting and talking, one of them left and the remaining ladies immediately began talking about the lady that left in a negative way and my mother got up and left. That was the last time she sat outside with the neighbors. She didn't like gossip, or being "two-faced," as she called it.

I was eight years old when my dad tried to move us into a larger apartment. He wanted to get us into the almost-completed Cathedral Housing Project. I later found out that it was really hard to get into the projects. Basically you had to know someone. Well, he went to see someone in City Hall and whatever they promised to do they didn't do. Finally, he went to see someone from the neighborhood, someone who had become well known in local politics, and within a few months we were moving on up Washington Street to the Cathedral Project. We were all so excited. The apartment was on

Singgie, Punchie, and Necie

the first floor and it had three bedrooms and a bathroom *inside* the apartment. It had a flushing toilet. I don't remember ever having seen anything like this before. Boy, we kids would stand around and flush and watch. My mother would say, "Stop before it gets stopped up." The kitchen had a gas stove. You turned the black button and fire came out. No need for coal or wood. No more sign in the window for the coal or woodman.

My mother was scared to death for us to be near that stove. Every five minutes she'd shout, "Get away from that stove" or "Come out of the kitchen." The street still had dirt roads and one of my brothers fell and cracked all his front teeth running around and playing on all the stacked up granite blocks that were going to be curbs. The priests and nuns from the church across the street came to visit and get to know the new parishioners and everyone knew Frank, the neighborhood policeman.

Slocum's five-and-dime was across the street, Kennedy's Butter & Eggs and "My Market" was a small local grocery store. There was the bakery on the corner of Dedham Street where we took our nickels to buy a lemon tart, or if you could muster up fifteen cents, a Bismarck, or cherry Cokes at the luncheonette.

The projects had areas safe for kids to play and ride bikes, and Blackstone Park was right across the street. My dad bought himself a beautiful Schwinn bicycle. It was maroon with chrome fenders and he decorated it with all the bells and whistles, fur streamers like raccoon tails that hung down from the handlebars, and I don't even remember what else, but this was his thing of beauty and he shined it up with chrome polish after every use. He went down to Police Station Four and got a license for it. Then he proceeded to get each of us a bike, for birthdays or for Christmas. We didn't all get them at the same time, but as each one got his or her bike, we all went to Police Station Four and got a license. We thought that was a really big thing. "Oh, someone's getting their license next week," we'd say. Then on some Sundays in good weather my dad led the bike brigade, and we would ride to the Esplanade or the Commons or to Fenway and whoever didn't yet have a bike would ride on Daddy's cross bar until the day they got their license.

Sunday was always family day. We got up and went to church. You couldn't even think about going out to play if you couldn't go to church. You always saw families walking in the street on Sunday, walking to and from church or to visit a family member or friends, all dressed up in their Sunday best and walking. Times were a lot safer back then.

The South End is so different now. My youngest sister moved out of state shortly after high school, about thirty years ago. She hasn't been home since 1998. She came for my mother's funeral, but she didn't get a chance to visit the old neighborhood or to see what Washington Street looks like without the el — how sunny and bright it can look on a good day — almost too much space. At first I wondered what in the world they were going to put there to use up some of the space. It looked so odd. I was afraid to cross the street. The projects still stand. Blackstone Park is still there and looks better than I remember it. All the stores are gone and some streets as well. Washington Street across from the church now has a restaurant with valet parking. St. Vincent de Paul is gone, and Dover Street is now Berkeley Street. Laconia Street is gone, John J. Williams Elementary School where I went in third grade is gone, but the Red Fez Restaurant is still there on Washington Street.

My parents are both gone now. Denise is gone and all the boys are gone; Bernard just passed away a few weeks ago at my home. All in all, I had a good life. I feel blessed.

Unforgettable Characters

LALLY AND HER DAD

Mary O'Keefe

Some people have the time to enjoy their grandfathers. Others, like me, can only enjoy their grandfathers' lives by the tales told to us, which we in turn give to our families. Daniel Saunders was my grandfather, and my mother told me so many stories about him. She told me that Dan was a *Boston Globe* reporter. When he was new on the job and covering a murder trial, he somehow found out the verdict before the jury foreman had handed it to the judge. As the judge announced the verdict of "guilty," the newsboy outside was already selling the papers with the guilty headline on top. The judge was upset, but Dan wouldn't give up his source, and so he went to jail along with the editor. This was before 1900, and my mother said he was the first reporter to go to jail for not revealing his source. Dan's next job was as a boxing reporter and editor. In his office, he welcomed anyone connected with the sport. He loved the champs, including Jack Dempsey. His favorite boxer was Sam Langford, the lightweight champ who was sometimes called "The Boston Bonecrusher" and "The Boston Terror" because he fought men far above his weight class and beat them. He and Dan were great friends. In fact, Dan accompanied Langford to New Orleans for a match, and rode in the back of the train with Langford in a car that was then known as the Jim Crow car, and Dan was arrested for riding in the back.

Although my grandfather was a successful writer, he had his struggles. His wife died of cancer when she was young. Her death left Dan with six children, between the ages of six and eighteen, including my mother who was twelve years old at the time. According to my mother, the first thing Dan did was go to St. Andrew's Church and take a pledge that he would never drink a drop of liquor again. It was a pledge he kept for the rest of his life, not that he was much of a drinker.

My mother was Dan's pet, in part because the doctors had told him that she was too frail and sickly to survive into adulthood. She was a tiny, sweet thing, who weighed just ninety pounds when I knew her. She had auburn hair that hung down below her waist. She was named Helen at birth, but then her name changed when her siblings nicknamed her Nellie. Then later on when one of my cousins couldn't pronounce Nellie, her nickname changed again to Lally, and that's all anybody called her after that.

Dan hired housekeepers to help with the housework, and then my mother took over for them when the last housekeeper retired. Sometimes she went to the bank to withdraw the money she needed for the shopping and bills. She told me that one time she was at the bank and she asked the bank manager to call Dan at the newspaper. At the time Dan happened to be sitting in his office talking to Jack Johnson, the first African American heavyweight champion and a national celebrity. According to my mother, Dan got off the phone with the bank and complained to Johnson that the manager thought Nellie shouldn't walk home alone with all that money. Without hesitation, Johnson said to Dan, "I'll keep an eye on her." And he did. She found out later that Johnson planned to walk a half block or so behind her so that she wouldn't know he was there. At her doorstep, my mother turned around and waved to him, and Johnson later told Dan that he thought he'd been so sneaky in following her. It was a story my mother told for the rest of her life.

Dan eventually became sick with throat cancer after all the years of covering boxing with the resins and smoke in the air. When Dan was very sick and in a great deal of pain, a friend of my mother's suggested that he would be more comfortable if he had a sip of brandy. The doctor agreed that brandy might help him feel better, but the doctor still warned her against it. "Nellie," he said, "He would never forgive you if you gave it to him. He swore he'd never take a drop." And so she never brought it up again.

Dan Saunders died on May 5, 1923. According to one obituary, he had been a *Boston Globe* reporter and editor for forty-three years, and had become one of the foremost boxing and sports writers in the country. Many famous boxers, athletes, and prominent businessmen attended his funeral. According to my mother, they locked his office door on the day he died and it was never used again.

After Dan died, the family house reverted to another owner. When my mother and father got married, they got an apartment, and three years later I was born there. My little brother, Albert Stewart, named after my father, was born six years later.

Ours was a great family for nicknames. My mother and father called each other "Hoak." One day my mother had extra money after doing the shopping, and she decided to buy a bicycle for each of her two nephews. When Dad came home he said, "Hoak! Where's the meat for dinner?" And she said, "Oh! No wonder I had that extra money." It didn't bother her at all that she'd spent the food money on something else. Money was nothing to my mother. I never heard her ask the price of anything and she never bought anything on sale. If she had a dollar, she had to spend it. Funny thing is that she never worked, never had a social security number, and never had any of her own money.

In our house, the food was always good. Both my father and mother were excellent cooks. One night Dad was making his great chicken pot pie in the big roasting pan. The smell told us that we were in for a treat. We heard him taking it out of the oven, and then we heard a bang. My aunt Celia and I ran to the kitchen, and there on the floor we saw the roasting pan and Dad bending over it. Both my aunt and I said, "It's okay," as we lifted the food off the floor. That night my Dad, my aunt, my brother, and I sat at the dinner table and watched Mom put food on everyone's plate. It was a very quiet meal. My aunt sat beside me, and I don't know how we kept from laughing. It had to be the look on Dad's face; I had never seen that look. But the next day even Dad had to laugh. I asked what the things floating around were and he said, "That was celery salt." My aunt looked at me and winked.

My mother had stayed close to her siblings because their mother had died when they were young. In my childhood, we were a very united family. There were three carloads of us going to the beach in the summer. Every five years we would go to Plymouth Beach, which was a special trip for us. We'd have an ice cream cake and every time one of my uncles would say that he had won the cake in a contest. It was years before we realized that they had bought the cake. We ate hard-boiled eggs at the beach, and I remember running past my uncle to break the eggs on his head. We laughed a lot and I still tell stories about the parties and trips to the beach, and our little jokes, and everything my mother told me about Dan, the grandfather I wish I'd known.

When Lally was little, the doctors said she would never survive, but she lived to be eighty-four years old. She came to live with my family for the last few years of her life. We all miss her. It would be great for everyone to have a Lally in their lives.

MY MOTHER NEVER IRONED

Dorothy Dorsey

My mother, Wilma Ann (Woods) Dorsey was not a traditional 1940s mother. She didn't bake; the Cushman's Bakery truck delivered three times a week. Reid Bros. Laundry picked up our dirty clothes on Saturday and brought them back cleaned and pressed on Tuesday. She didn't grocery shop; my dad did the shopping. She did one thing that most of the neighborhood ladies did not: she drove. We had a black Nash automobile that she drove frequently, especially to visit her parents in Taunton. She was very independent. And she was beautiful. With her blond hair and blue eyes, everyone said she looked like the movie actress Jean Harlow.

My mother did cook — with a lot of canned food. Spaghetti night was a special treat, a Chef Boyardee boxed spaghetti dinner. It came in a tall, thin box containing dry spaghetti, a can of sauce, and a little can of grated cheese. Another one of Mom's special dinners was a whole cooked chicken in a can — Banquet Chicken, 1950s convenience. We ate baked potatoes every night, along with a canned veggie and meat except on Friday nights when fish was on the menu. If we didn't like what was being served for dinner, she would simply say, "This is not a hotel where there would be many choices. This is what is being served here tonight." She cooked all meals except for Sunday dinner, which my father prepared. He insisted upon using the newest kitchen appliance, which at that time was a pressure cooker. I was always afraid that it would explode and, sure enough, one Sunday it did. We had squash all over the kitchen walls and ceiling.

Wilma Ann Woods Dorsey, 1934

When I was in grammar school, I was a very chubby little girl. My mother was ahead of her time in her thinking that it was not good for a child to be overweight, so she took me to the doctor and they put me on a weight-loss program with the promise of a beautiful First Communion dress, regular-sized, not from the "chubbette" section of Jordan Marsh's children's department. She worked so hard: she ordered only skim milk from the Hood's milkman, she bought the canned peaches in heavy syrup and washed them under cold water to get all the syrup off, and she tried hiding the Cushman Bakery products from me, but that didn't work well so she stopped the bakery order for a few months. I did get thinner and fit into that regular-sized First Communion dress, as promised.

Sundays, either for dinner or after dinner, we would drive to Taunton to visit my grandparents. The trip took longer in those days and we always stayed too late. My mother never wanted to leave. My sister Barbara and I would fall asleep on my grandparents' beds until my father would awaken us and guide us, half asleep, to the car. On the way home, without fail, we would run into heavy traffic on Route 138 when the Taunton Dog Track was just letting out, making the ride home to Hyde Park even longer.

My mother was not a coffee klatch type of person. She was friendly with the other women in our neighborhood, but was not one to sit in a neighbor's kitchen to chat for hours. After she got us off to school, she would sit down with her cup of Nescafé instant coffee and read the *Boston Herald,* her morning ritual. If I got up late at night, I would see her curled up on the couch in the living room reading the evening edition of the *Boston Traveler.*

One of her good friends, Phyllis, lived next door. She and Phyllis were very much alike. Among other things, they both liked politics, the Red Sox, and the soap *As the World Turns*. My mother listened to the Red Sox games on the radio until we got a black and white TV in 1948. I would come home from school to find her watching the game. She got her love of baseball from her father and I guess I have inherited my love of it from her.

Friday was housecleaning day. Mom would get out the carpet sweeper, furniture polish, and the Windex and get to work. On occasion she would drive to Taunton to hire Ruby, the woman who cleaned her mother's house, and bring her back to Boston to do some heavy cleaning. She then had to turn around and drive Ruby back to Taunton at night. It was worth it to her, or so she said.

In 1952, my sister Gail was born. What a wonderful surprise this was for Barbara and me. I was eleven and she was nine. When our mother was in St. Elizabeth's Hospital, we pooled our allowance and bought a Ming tree (also known as a bonsai tree) for her. In those days, children were not allowed into the hospital during visiting hours so our father delivered the Ming tree for us. My mother wrote a letter from the hospital thanking us for the Ming tree and telling us all about our new sister. I still have that letter.

Life went along all right for us until July 1955. My mother was in bed sick for two days with a very bad headache and fever. On the second day, she bumped her arm against the headboard and her arm went limp. She said she couldn't feel anything in it. I remember watching my father walk her down the back stairs on the way to the hospital. She wore a tan two-piece summer dress with purple roosters on it. I never saw her walk again. The diagnosis was polio. She was forty years old.

I entered my freshman year of high school that fall at Notre Dame Academy in Roxbury. My mother had been in the hospital since that July day with no hope of coming home soon. I was fourteen, Barbara was twelve, and Gail was three. We were not allowed into the hospital at all and any adults who visited had to wear masks and gowns. Some days, instead of going directly home after school, I would take the elevated train in the opposite direction to Northampton

Station in Roxbury. I'd walk to City Hospital, locate my mother's building, climb the fire escape, and talk to her through the closed window. She always wanted me to leave before it got too late so I'd say goodbye, throw her a kiss, and walk all the way back to the Northampton train station in tears.

Eventually, she came home to stay. With the exception of a short visit at Christmas, she had been gone for over a year. She was paralyzed except for her right arm, which worked well enough to allow her to feed herself and turn the pages of the newspaper. Even though she couldn't move, she was very much in charge. I can still hear her saying, "Someone put the potatoes in!" Over the following ten years, there were many things she had me doing in her stead. One year at Easter time, she insisted I drive all the way out to Shopper's World in Framingham to get a special hat for Gail that she saw advertised in the paper. I got lost and what should have been a forty-five minute trip took two hours. She had me doing all sorts of things like that; it just drove me crazy! But, I did them. Trimming the Christmas tree was another project. Barbara and I decorated it under my mother's explicit direction. I was thankful that Christmas came only once a year.

When I think of it now, I cannot imagine how terrible it must have been for her to lose the active, independent life she was accustomed to and become dependent on so many people just to get through the day. She died at the age of fifty, in 1965. My mother was a wonderful, loving, smart, and funny woman. I would give anything to have her back for just one day.

MEMORIES OF KENNY WEST

Ralph Cairns

T he happiest year in my life was probably 1971. I had recently moved to the South End, which bears little resem-
blance to the South End of today with its rehabbing and
revitalization. I was working at University Hospital, which is now
part of the Boston Medical Center. At that time I was an employee in
the messenger service, now called transport. One snowy morning,
I was working on the Special Care Unit (SCU) where I met a man
who would become a dear friend, Kenneth R. West. He was lying
on a stretcher recuperating from kidney transplant surgery. Even
then, he was making plans to get well and climb Mt. Washington.

Kenny's positive outlook was inspiring to me. We bonded right
away. We would talk and talk. As he got better, I pushed him in
his wheelchair. Then, finally, he just needed the IV pole on wheels.
I ran his errands outside the hospital including getting his favorite brand of smokes (Parliaments) and cheese crackers with peanut butter. We would meet clandestinely in the stairwell outside the
SCU so he could smoke. The nurses overlooked it so long as I kept

his smokes. I know this would never happen today because times have changed.

Kenny and I were as different as two people could be. He was very athletic, with a lean, well-muscled frame, approximately six foot two, and always well groomed with nary a thing out of place. He smelled of Old Spice, Dunkin Donuts, and probably those Parliaments. He was well read but not educated beyond high school. I was short, balding, uncoordinated, and overweight, not in any sense athletic. "Laurel and Hardy" is probably an apt description of how we looked together.

Kenny was a Type A personality, meaning his mind and body were always racing along to another point. He had a big, kind heart and his soul was full of forgiveness. He was also very mischievous (like when smoking his Parliaments in the hospital stairwell). Though I never climbed Mt. Washington with him, we enjoyed walking Castle Island and some of the Walk for Hunger together. That hill at the ten-mile point always did me in, but Kenny, after catching his breath, would only be more motivated to finish the twenty miles. He liked exploring historical Boston, Quincy, and my hometown of Portsmouth, New Hampshire. Together we found the original location of the infamous old Howard Theater in Scollay Square and the United First Parish Church in Quincy, where many members of the Adams family are buried. We would walk on Peirce Island, Portsmouth's version of Castle Island. Walking, exploring, and reading. We loved playing word games, trying to use the word *faux* or *ubiquitous* in a sentence that made sense was enlightening and amusing to us. We would try to stump each other with new words.

We were pals through thick and thin — even at his end in 1993 when his kidney failed, his heart slowed and slowed, and his Type A personality was gone. Of course those Parliaments were all his ruin. I miss him. I never really got a good chance to say good-bye. I just sat at his bedside crying for him and probably for myself. Somehow part of my life was over. I no longer thought of myself as young.

A friend said that Kenny was like Peter Pan: he never really grew up. So I'll close this essay by saying that Kenny *did* change before his untimely death. He met Betsy and her young children. He loved her with every breath he took. She would often join us in our exploring and walking, enjoying each other's company. He changed in his heart and soul, if not so much in his general behavior. Kenny was a wonderful rogue of a character, but also a principled person with an innate sense of goodness and integrity.

Kenny, I sign off by that big clock on the wall with a song sung by Billie Holiday, "I'll be seeing you, in all the old familiar places that this heart of mine embraces."

December 1, 2011

Kenny,

On this bright clean morning, you will remember that I am an agnostic, a person who never had faith in much of anything other than the transforming power of love. There is a still a big part of me that hopes upon hope there is another side: not hell, maybe not even heaven, but another side not yet comprehensible to me.

So this morning as I sit in my rocking chair looking upon SoWa, I wish you were sitting here too with your Parliaments. Just what in the hell happened from 1971 until this late fall morning? Maybe we will meet again someday.

WHAT BROKE AND
WHO BROKE IT

Judith Klau

T he vase was alabaster white and looked like a lady with no head and no legs. It was about fifteen inches high with a bulbous bottom and a handle on either side from the waist to the top, like a Greek amphora. When I drew it in response to the command "draw a vase" in third grade, the teacher said that no vase had two handles like that, but she was wrong.

Mr. and Mrs. DeAngelo had brought the vase from Italy and given it to my mother. They were the tenants who lived on the first floor of the two-family house owned by my grandparents in East Hartford. The DeAngelos were "other," I somehow knew, because like the Hopkins family next door and Junior MacSweeney across the street, they were not Jewish. This consciousness came very early in my life and colors almost everything I think and do and am, but didn't have much to do with the vase, except that my mother valued it highly.

She kept it on a tall, three-legged mahogany pedestal that stood in our living room next to the piano. I hated that piano so much that I used to bite the wooden music desk when I was supposed to be practicing. So, I knew the vase well from those bored quarter-hours.

Every year in the late spring, my mother called a carpet service to take up the heavy wine-colored wool rugs and put down sisal rugs for the summer. These gentlemen also put slipcovers on the furniture including cretonne leggings for the piano that closed with tiny little snaps that — like the garters on my mother's corset — never closed all the way down. When I should have been practicing, I lay under the piano and tried for hours to close them.

One year my father decided while my mother was out that he would undertake the changing of the carpets with my help. I must have been five or six. He stationed me next to the pedestal while he got ready to pull the rug from underneath it. I carefully held on to the stem of the pedestal, but when he yanked the rug, the vase flew off the top and crashed heavily into another vase standing on the brick hearth of the fireplace. They both shattered.

My father's look of astonishment astonished me! He hadn't told me to hold the vase, so I didn't. He sat on the floor for a moment thinking and then said, "Go upstairs and get into bed and don't come down. Let me deal with Mother." It was about three o'clock in the afternoon. I learned later that he said that I had broken both vases. It was the first time that I realized my father feared my mother's explosive tendencies. And so I always forgave him when he used me as a human shield.

*My father Harry Rulnick dancing at my wedding
on March 9, 1957*

You have to understand that my mother — who at her best was a
funny, handsome, card-playing lady — had married my irrepress-
ible dad to escape her asthmatic, irritable father. She came from a
large family, but I believe everyone was careful of her because of
her fierce temper. Hearing my mother in full tirade forever scarred
a college roommate of mine; Mother didn't care who heard her, and
you never knew what would set her off.

There was another incident when my father wanted to show my sister and me the miraculous properties of a new product called Reddi-Whip, whipped cream that flew out of a can when you depressed a little gadget on top. Unfortunately he chose the dining room for his experiment. My mother had just had the dining room ceiling rejiggered, with a ceiling soffit under which lights had been mounted. This whole operation was her beloved decorator's biggest and most expensive feat. However, both ceiling and walls had been prepared before painting with a linen underlayment, and when he squirted, the stuff went straight up to the ceiling and spread out into a huge greasy stain right on the soffit. When she saw it, my mother was horrified, but my father told her, "Judy did it." I was outside playing, and by the time I came in, she had calmed down so I missed the full nightmare display.

This decorator, who loomed large in my childhood because she and her bills were a source of friction between my parents, had also determined that every piece of furniture in my sister's bedroom had to be painted the exact shade of leaf-green that figured in the bedspread and curtains. The upstairs telephone was in my sister's room, and lacking paper, my father once jotted a telephone number on the nightstand in permanent ink. I got blamed for that one, too.

My father never met a story he didn't want to tell or a person whose name he could remember. So why did I love my father so much given these peccadilloes? I think because he loved me so much and showed it. I was incredibly proud of him. He was the father who took the kids in the neighborhood to the amusement park, gave us money for the rides, and waited in the Keno parlor until we had had enough. He was the father who proudly stopped by to see me at college with the men from his work when they were at a convention in Boston. He was the guy who presided at meetings of my mother's family circle as favored son- and brother-in-law. He was the father who led the Passover Seders at my maternal grandmother's house after my grandfather died even though there were four sons in that house.

Many years after my father had died, his youngest brother died. He was the last of those six children who had come to this country and traveled very different paths. My uncle, a public accountant, had been both an educated man and also a man who devoted himself to Jewish learning. He was the *gabbai* (an exalted role in the Torah service) in his synagogue. My father, who loved Judaism but was largely unschooled, never had the honors of my Uncle Morris. It is one of my fondest memories that his wife, my Aunt Sarah, who was herself a member of Phi Beta Kappa and a Jewish scholar, said to me at my uncle's funeral, "Your father was also an *adam kadosh*," a holy man.

MY MOTHER'S SECRET LIFE

Loura White

My mother was five foot three. This was one of the few things I know about her. She had a dancer's legs and she used them to move very fast. When she wanted to entertain me, she would kick one leg over her head and say, "Eat your oatmeal" in pig Latin. This phrase would make me collapse with laughter every time.

My mother was small and very thin. Her hair was red and she wore a pageboy bob. She had hyperthyroidism, a condition that made her metabolism work overtime. She told me she had her thyroid taken out twice, but it always grew back. Because she was so thin, she had many formulas for gaining weight. Her goal was to reach one hundred pounds. One formula was 7-Up and cream for breakfast. She hated it. Another time she drank beer for breakfast, along with huge bowls of oatmeal. None of these worked, and her energy was constant. Looking back, I think she moved so fast and so much she burned up all she ate and drank.

What she drank was black coffee. She took a quart thermos to the office and came home briefly at noon to refill it. When she got home at night, she would take off her hat and gloves and high heels, put on another pair of high heels — because she couldn't wear flats — and make a pot of coffee. Then she could smoke, too. She was always reading a book. The three were a trio — book, cigarette, coffee. Men adored her and she treated them like dirt.

My mother never spoke of my father, or their marriage, or the family from which she was estranged. Whenever I asked about my father, she would cry, and sometimes become hysterical. So I stopped asking. Was I curious? Yes, but there was an insurmountable wall when I asked. My mother was quite a character and she kept a lot of secrets, including her age. Every time I asked about her past, her answer was the same: "None of your business." And yet, she couldn't keep all of her secrets to herself.

There were just the two of us: my mother, the single parent, and me, the only child. Her unbreakable rule — one of many — was that we must live in a house. She said it was because of me, but looking back, I wonder if it wasn't primarily because she needed a garage. Not for her car, as it was always parked in the driveway, but for storage. She had trunks, boxes, and just about anything that could be filled, and filled they were. No garage was big enough. Whenever we moved, all the trunks moved with us. I was told to stay out of the garage, and never to open any of the trunks. "And I will know if you do!" she told me.

I believed her, but then one day I went in the garage anyway. I was just learning to read handwriting, and I was bolder. Fearful and determined, I opened one trunk. There was a signed photograph of Rudolf Valentino and many letters all bound. The top one was written in green ink.

Fascinated by this letter, I opened it. My project was to decipher the handwriting. It was difficult but one phrase I understood was, "Please don't teach the baby to hate me." The letter was signed, "Bob." That phrase terrified me. I realized that the letter had been written by my father, who had died when I was twenty months old. He had died of pneumonia in 1932 at the age of twenty-eight.

I quickly put the letter back into its envelope, closed the trunk, and left the garage. The phrase haunted me. I felt a shock when it dawned on me that I was the baby he wrote about. I was moved by the understanding that my father knew about me and cared what I thought of him. The only trace of him was in my baby book, a sepia photo of him holding me wrapped like a huge bundle as he came out of the Los Angeles Maternity Cottage.

I also saw business cards in that trunk, and I realized they had belonged to my father. One advertised sightseeing trips over the Bay Area in an airplane. You could get a fifteen-minute ride for two dollars. That's how I learned that my father and his friend had run this business, and that my father had been a pilot. All I know about him was in this trunk, in my baby book. And then of course, there were times when my mother's brother (who I've always called "my drinking uncle") would get tipsy and divulge details about my father, who had been his best friend. My uncle did this to enrage his sister. He told me that she had been a dancer and that she and my father had danced in contests up and down the California coast.

Because she was a single parent, my mother had to work very hard. Yet she never went to her job without hat and gloves. She never, to my knowledge, rode a bus. She was a single mother with one child, but she never felt deprived.

I picture my mother always with a cigarette in her mouth. As she cooked, the ash would drop into the food. I don't remember her ever smelling of smoke or nicotine. Her cooking was always delicious. I still don't know why everything she cooked was so good. Her grilled cheese sandwiches were a special treat on Saturdays because she only worked a half-day on Saturday. She wore a cologne called Blue Grass, and I loved the fragrance.

I don't remember much until we lived at 347 North Seventh Avenue. There was a fence made of iron bars outside, and I would swing on these bars. Franklin D. Roosevelt was a secular sacred name in our little bungalow. During the Depression the WPA saved us; that and my mother's fierce determination. When she needed a job, she applied as a waitress. She stood in line with seventy-two other women for a chance to work for tips even though she had no experience as a waitress. The woman who hired her, Fran from Texas, became her close friend. Years later, Fran said to me, "To this day, I don't know why I hired her. But she was a damn good worker."

My mother also signed up for typing lessons, five nights a week because she wanted to work in an office. When she took the typing classes I stayed home alone. She would set the alarm for my bedtime and say, "When this rings, you go inside, brush your teeth, and go to bed, and I'll know if you don't. Mrs. Cotton will look in on you and see you're all right." Mrs. Cotton was a terribly old (to me) neighbor across the court. I could see her and her daughter, Maple, as I sat on the tiny cement porch, drawing pictures by the porch light. I never heard my mother come home. When she finished the course, she said, "Thank you, FDR." She entered the typing pool but didn't stay long. A secretary no-showed one day and that was the start of my mother's climb through the office world. She later worked for an electric company, and whenever she joined an office, she soon became the manager. Her manager, meanwhile, left for the golf course while my mother ran the electrical business.

During the years my mother worked in an office, a group of women played cards every week at our house. They started out playing bridge, but someone, perhaps her friend Fran, taught my mother and aunt to play poker, and this changed everything. They played for matches and sometimes had beer. Where the money for cigarettes came from was no one's business, but they all smoked and laughed and laughed. They put me to sleep in my mother's double bed, and I would go to sleep to the raucous sound of their laughter. Later they moved me to the sofa, where I slept.

I always thought of my mother as a formidable force, rather than a person. It wasn't until I was older that I learned my mother had a past. My uncle told me that she had been married before she married my dad. When I was fourteen I learned that my father had also been married before and that I had a half-brother, Kenneth. We

SOUTH END

learned that my father's brother had died intestate and that Kenneth and I had both inherited money. My mother was the guardian of my estate and paid for my college and expenses from it. Whenever I needed anything for school, my mother would say, "Well, I think the estate can cover this if you buy it used," as she wrote out a check for me.

On the day I turned twenty-one my mother disappeared from my life, taking whatever was left of my inheritance with her. I never saw her again, and the rest of her secrets she kept to herself.

About the Authors

CLAIRE BANATT ("Happy Trails," page 144) has lived in Hyde Park all her life, went through the local schools, and went on to work at several places—including Eastman Kodak, Stoneham Webster, Dr. Brown (an allergist), and Boston Lying-In Hospital. She married Ed Banatt and after being married for ten years, went back to work for the Commonwealth of Massachusetts. Claire and Ed have been married for forty-seven years. They have four children and seven grandchildren.

SHEBA (BROWN) BARBOZA ("An Enduring Love," page 6) was born in Charlottesville, Virginia, in 1936 to Russell and Leila (Forrest) Brown, the fifth of seven children. In 1949, her mother moved Sheba and her two younger brothers to Roxbury, where relatives had settled years before. She graduated from Girls' High School of Boston, earned a certificate in key punch operation, and took night courses at Boston College. Sheba worked a number of jobs while raising her son, Stanley, Jr., and retired in 1998. She has lived in the Hyde Park area for more than thirty years. Her sisters are gone, but she has three brothers left—Percy, James, and Arthur. "I appreciate Mayor Menino and the City of Boston for all the senior activities offered. The *Memoir Project* has been a once-in-a-lifetime opportunity. Special thanks to GrubStreet, Michelle Seaton, and all the coaches. I could never have done this without you!"

CAROL BLAIR ("Girl Engineer," page 167) lives with her husband, a fellow adventurer, on the border of the South End and Roxbury and manages their three-family building. She enjoys the rich opportunities of Boston and loves creating Urban Adventures for Seniors. For Carol, life is an adventure: from walking, hiking, cycling, and yoga to singing with the Old South Church choir and the Platinum Singers at Tubman House; from spending time with her grandchildren to delving into her family's history (and writing about it).

EILEEN ROACH BRADLEY ("Keep Calm and Carry On," page 64) was born in Lynn, Massachusetts, in 1926. She moved to Roxbury in 1931 and married Peter Bradley in 1950. She and her husband bought a home in West Roxbury where they raised five children and have been married for sixty-one years. Eileen is an avid gardener. She has traveled to Europe, Ireland, England, and across America. A typical West Roxbury housewife, she also summers on the Cape. On Tuesdays, you can find her at Twin River Casino spending her children's inheritance.

ITA BRIDGES ("Leaving Home," page 208) was born in Roscommon, Ireland. She immigrated to Boston in 1948 and married her husband in 1950. Because her husband was in the navy, she traveled with him for ten years to France and England, returning to Boston in 1961. There she studied for her LN through the City of Boston at Trade High School for Girls. She has five children and three grandchildren. She and her husband were married for fifty-six years.

RALPH CAIRNS ("Memories of Kenny West," page 240) was born in 1942 in the Puddle Dock neighborhood of Portsmouth, New Hampshire. He moved to the South End in 1971 and worked at University Hospital for twenty-five years. He resides today at St. Helena's House in the South End. Now retired, Ralph enjoys writing and going to the movies.

Born in 1925 in Dorchester, JACK CASEY ("The Johnson Nursing Home," page 72) moved to West Roxbury when he was a year old and still lives there. His paternal grandparents were from Ireland and his maternal grandparents were born here. Jack graduated from Boston Latin School and Boston College and served three years in the army, mostly in Japan and Hawaii, from 1943 to 1946. He volunteers with recent immigrants and a group learning English as a second language.

MARION FENNELL CONNOLLY ("Life in a Tenement," page 57) was born in the Boston City Hospital, on February 17, 1933, the eldest of five children of Irish-born parents. Her childhood was spent in St. Patrick, St. Joseph, and St. Francis de Sales parishes, all in Roxbury. She graduated from Cathedral High School in Boston. At the age of fifty-one, she received an associate's degree from Labouré College and worked as a registered nurse. She was married forty-seven years to her husband, Marty, and raised six children in West Roxbury. She has eighteen grandchildren and one great-granddaughter.

DOROTHY DORSEY ("My Mother Never Ironed," page 234) was born in 1941. She has been a lifelong resident of Boston, spending her grammar school years in Hyde Park, and from high school on in West Roxbury. She retired from her administrative position at the Leland Home in Waltham. Dorothy has volunteered with the Elderly Services Division of Catholic Charities in their Friendly Visitor Program, the

Activities Department of the Deutsches Altenheim Nursing Home, and Faulkner Hospital. Her partner of thirty-three years, Jack Harrington, passed away in 2012. Together they were enthusiastic fans of the Red Sox, Celtics, and Patriots.

RAVEN ELLIOTT ("An Educated Woman," page 152) was born in 1920 in Greensboro, North Carolina, the daughter of a dentist and a teacher. She graduated from Fisk University in 1942 and earned her master's in biochemistry in 1944. She worked as a chemist at the Ford Motor Company and as a chemistry teacher. She married Adolph Elliott in 1946, and they were married sixty-one years until his death in 2007. They have one daughter.

KATHRYN M. FAIRBANKS ("In the Direction of Dreams," page 174) is a graduate of Emmanuel College in Boston, and lives in Roslindale. She taught elementary grades in the Boston Public Schools for thirty-five years. Since 1973, Kathy's avocation has been New England archaeology, as both a student and volunteer, and she has participated in digs at Capernaum and Beth Saida in the Holy Land as well. She currently serves as librarian for the Massachusetts Archaeological Society in Middleborough.

PATRICIA A. GEARY ("The Neighborhood," page 137) was born in 1938 in Brighton and is one of seven children of Irish immigrants. In 1982, she graduated from Boston College. Most of her career has been spent working in the medical profession. She currently volunteers at the Literacy Connection teaching English to newly arrived immigrants and helping them prepare for their citizenship examinations. She has a passion for traveling, particularly to London, and feels that she probably lived there in a prior life.

LEO ALEXANDER GILLIS ("A Story of Survival," page 194) was born in the Savin Hill section of Dorchester in 1939 to Leo Angus and Christine Isabelle Gillis, both of whom spoke Gaelic. Leo was the fourth of six children. Leo earned his GED in the 1970s and worked for the City of Boston for twenty-three years taking 9-1-1 calls. He is divorced and has four daughters and three grandchildren, two boys and a girl. He retired in 2002 and enjoys playing Scrabble and poker.

ROBERT GODINO ("The Toughest Job I Ever Loved," page 91) was born in 1935 in West Roxbury the first of nine children, which instilled in him the values of responsibility and volunteerism. He graduated from Roslindale High School in 1953 and joined the U.S. Navy during the Korean War. After his service tour, he graduated from college and enrolled in law school. From 1962 to 1964 he was a Peace Corps volunteer in the Dominican Republic. He was active in community affairs as a candidate for state representative, a Ward 20 delegate to state Democratic conventions for more than twenty years, soccer league coach, father of three sons, member of local community organizations, and producer/director of *West Roxbury Today*, a weekly public access TV program for more than eighteen years. Now retired, he is interested in preserving local recollections.

JUDI GORSUCH ("Waitress in the Sky," page 160), born in 1943 in Detroit, Michigan, came of age when women did not have varied careers. She spent two years in the 1960s teaching middle school. She went on to become a flight attendant for twenty years. She lives in Boston with her cat and memories of exciting travel.

BETSAIDA GUTIÉRREZ ("Following in Papa's Footsteps," page 78) was born in Puerto Rico and came to Boston in 1972. She has worked tirelessly with JNDC and City Life/Vida Urbana. She was the lead organizer in the creation of three other resident-led housing cooperatives in the neighborhood and created the program, *Latinos Comprando Casas,* for first-time homebuyers in the Latino community.

DELORES HALL ("Dolls and My Childhood Memories," page 42) was born in Harlem, New York City. After the completion of her schooling, she moved to Boston, where she worked as a seamstress, housewife, and a machinist. Later she trained to become a paraprofessional for the Boston Public Schools. She worked for twenty-one years before retiring. She currently resides in Boston where she shares her passion for dolls with others.

SHERRARD MOWRY HAMILTON ("Teaching at the Burke," page 99) was born in 1943 in Madison, Wisconsin. She grew up in Evanston, Illinois, and moved to the Boston area in 1972. For ten years she worked as English teacher before moving on to other careers. She is a co-founder and steering committee member of the Rainbow Lifelong Learning Institute, which offers courses to seniors. Sherrard is passionately political with a particular interest in the local food movement and working to stop the causes of climate change. She has a daughter and son-in-law, and two grandsons.

GAIL JACOBS ("A Love of Music," page 28) was born in Cambridge, Massachusetts, in 1940, and moved with her family to Brighton in 1943. She graduated from Brighton High School in 1957 and married Bill Jacobs in 1959. They had two children, and raised them in Brighton. She was active in the community and now lives in Watertown. She has two grandchildren and still loves music.

ILENE KATZ ("Changes," page 214) was born August 10, 1950 in Brooklyn, New York, to Frances and Abraham Katz. In 1952, her family moved into a brand-new Marine Park/Sheepshead Bay co-op, where Ilene lived with her parents, grandmother, and older brother, Mark. Ilene graduated from Sheepshead Bay High School in 1967 and attended City College, where she graduated with an associate's degree in merchandising. For several years, she worked in retail merchandising in Manhattan and Brooklyn, but eventually stopped working to care for her ailing mother. In 2004, Ilene moved to Boston so that her brother and sister-in-law could help her with her own health issues. Since Valentine's Day 2006, Ilene has lived in West Roxbury where she is active in the Friends of the West Roxbury Library.

JANICE BEALS KELLY ("Bubbles the Clown," page 83) was born on September 21, 1938, the day of the Great New England Hurricane. She lived in Cambridge for thirty years. She worked for Boston Gas Company from 1960 to 1999. She's lived in West Roxbury since 1975. Janice participates in a lot of programs at Ethos with her friends Marion and Anne.

SANDY KILBRIDE ("A Dream Fulfilled," page 129) was born in 1936 in the North End. When she was six years old, her family moved to Brighton. She was married and had four children when she left Brighton and moved to Florida. When her children were grown, she and her husband left Florida for Hawaii, where she spent twenty years before returning to her childhood home in Brighton. She now has seven grandchildren and three great-grandchildren, is active in the community, and enjoys gardening and dancing.

JUDITH KLAU ("On Sports," page 126, and "What Broke and Who Broke It," page 245), who now fulfills a lifelong dream by living in Boston, was born in Springfield, Massachusetts, in 1935 to parents who emigrated as children from Belarus (Russia/Poland). She graduated from Wellesley College, earned a master's in literature in 1971, and has been happily immersed in literature since then, teaching at several independent schools in New York and California, finally landing in Massachusetts at Groton School from which she retired in 1998. She has two married children and two grandchildren on the West Coast, but her true home is in Boston's South End.

ANNE MAHONEY ("How the Red Sox Captured My Heart," page 14), the oldest of five, was born and raised in Brighton, and except for a few years in her twenties has always lived there. She worked for forty-five years with various firms in Boston, retiring after thirty-nine years as an executive assistant with the accounting firm of Ernst & Young. She is now enjoying retirement by volunteering, gardening, reading, and spending time with friends and family.

MARY A. McCARTHY ("Yes: A Story of Love," page 3, and "My Father's Gift to Me," page 122) was born in Brighton in 1942, the oldest of five children. She still lives in her family home in Oak Square with her beloved Liz and their two cats. She is a teacher and healer and loves interviewing people to learn about their lives and to hear their stories. She enjoys extended family gatherings and celebrations, sharing meals with friends, working in the community, gardening, family history, and sitting on the porch chatting with neighbors. She and Liz have been "greening" their home by creating a rain garden, installing solar hot water, and making plans for solar electric. They are also committed composters and recyclers.

GEORGE "CHIP" McCORMACK ("I'll See You at Ma's," page 34) was born in 1929 at St. Elizabeth Hospital in Brighton. He was the youngest of seven children born to Bernard and Marguerite McCormack. He grew up at Westford Place, commonly called "the Alley." George graduated from Brighton High in 1946 and became a machinist. In the service, he became an aircraft mechanic. He married Mary Lou Carey McCormack in 1957 and they were together for forty-seven wonderful years until Mary Lou died of cancer in 2003. They had six daughters and a son, and have twelve grandchildren and one great-grandchild, so far.

JOHN MOWLES ("The Pirates," page 116) was born and raised in the Neponset section of Dorchester and resided there until marriage. He went to local schools and Boston Technical High School. He has three sons and seven grandchildren. After service in the U.S. Navy, he became a police officer and retired as a Detective Captain. John is currently retired and living the good life.

NANCY O'HARA ("Brown-Eyed Girl," page 20) was born in Framingham in 1942. She has lived in Brighton with her husband, Michael, since 1976. She earned her BA, BS, and MA from Emmanuel College, Boston State College, and Boston College, respectively. Nancy retired from the Boston Public Schools after a career in the English department and as school librarian at East Boston High School. She volunteers at Boston Community Leadership Academy and the Brighton-Allston Historical Society and Heritage Museum, and is active with 57 Readers and Writers, a neighborhood group which performs twice a year at the Faneuil Branch Library in Oak Square.

MARY O'KEEFE ("Lally and Her Dad," page 228) was born in Forest Hills in 1925 to Helen Teresa Saunders and Albert Stewart Olsen. She moved to West Roxbury with her parents in 1931. She married Paul Edward O'Keefe, "the handsomest guy you've ever seen," on July 17, 1948, and they had three children, Albert, Paula, and Thomas. Mary passed away in the spring of 2013.

DOROTHY PERRYMAN ("Sun from Another Garden: My Journey from Georgia to Boston and Beyond," page 200) was born in Madison, Georgia, on May 19, 1944, to sharecropper parents, Freddie and Fannie Perryman. She grew up in a family of three children. The family migrated to Boston in 1949. She graduated from Girls' High School in Roxbury in 1962. In 1979, she earned a bachelor's in sociology from the University of Massachusetts. She earned a master's in pastoral ministry in 1995 at Marygrove College in Detroit, Michigan. She is currently a resident of Boston.

EDY REES ("Finding Heaven in the Woods of Maine," page 108) was born in 1942 at the Faulkner Hospital. When she was one year old, her family moved from Codman Square (Dorchester) to Westwood, where she grew up. She holds a bachelor's degree in English literature from Boston University and a master's in education from State College at Boston. She also has several post-master's certificates. Edy worked as a ghostwriter for the American Physical Society. She was a tenant organizer in New York City, where she raised her two children, Megan and Colin; a bereavement counselor and case manager for homeless people living with HIV/AIDS in New York; and a counselor at the Labouré Center of Catholic Charities in South Boston, retiring in 2009. Edy is now a busy stay-at-home grandmother, gardener, and community activist in Roslindale.

EILEEN WALSH SAWYER ("I Thought We Had Everything, But We Didn't Have Much," page 50) was born at the Boston Lying-In Hospital to William and Lauretta Walsh. She was educated by the Sisters of St. James at St. Columbkille School, Brighton. After graduation, she worked for AT&T until marriage. She became a military wife, U.S. Air Force, and after a tour of duty, returned to Brighton. She retired from Delta Elevator in Allston and has been a hospice volunteer for fifteen years. She is most proud of her four children and amazing thirteen grandchildren.

DOLORES "SINGGIE" JOHNSON SEAY ("Life is Good," page 219) was born in Boston's lower Roxbury in 1943. At age eight, she moved to Boston's South End. She attended Boston public schools and earned her GED. She retired from the New England Telephone Company after twenty-seven years. During this time, she earned her bachelor's in business management from Boston State College, married, and had two daughters, Nequesha Jennifer and India Madree. She has lived in the Roslindale/Hyde Park area since 1973 and now has four grandchildren: S'keira, Octavious, Dreamer, and London. When she's not reading, she enjoys music, movies, plays, travel, and spending time with her grandkids.

PATRICIA M. WALSH ("From Boston to Iran: A Peace Corps Education," page 183), a longtime Brighton resident before moving to West Roxbury, is the daughter of Irish immigrants. She graduated from Emmanuel College and earned a master's degree in journalism from Boston University. She was a reporter for the *Boston Globe* before joining the Peace Corps in Iran, Morocco, and Washington, D.C., and was the editor of the Suffolk University and Simmons College alumni magazines. She is a strong supporter of public libraries and public transportation.

LOURA WHITE ("My Mother's Secret Life," page 250) was born in Los Angeles Maternity Cottage in 1931. She spent much of her childhood in Phoenix and then San Diego, where she attended San Diego State College. She married in 1959 and moved to New York. In 1969 she moved to Indonesia where she lived for eighteen years before moving to Turkey for seven years. She now lives in Boston.

For Further Reading

BOOKS ABOUT WRITING MEMOIR

Abercrombie, Barbara. *Courage and Craft: Writing Your Life into Story*. Novato, CA: New World Library, 2007.

Barrington, Judith. *Writing the Memoir: From Truth to Art*. Portland, OR: The Eighth Mountain Press, 2002.

Goldberg, Natalie. *Old Friend from Far Away: The Practice of Writing Memoir*. New York: Free Press, 2008.

Gutkind, Lee. *You Can't Make This Stuff Up: The Complete Guide to Writing Creative Nonfiction — from Memoir to Literary Journalism and Everything in Between*. Da Capo, 2012.

Kephart, Beth. *Handling the Truth: On the Writing of Memoir*. New York: Gotham, 2013.

Ledoux, Denis. *Turning Memories into Memoirs: A Handbook for Writing Lifestories*. Lisbon Falls, ME: Soleil Press, 2005.

Lippincott, Sharon M. *The Heart and Craft of Lifestory Writing: How to Transform Memories into Meaningful Stories*. Pittsburgh, PA: Lighthouse Point Press, 2007.

Miller, Lynn C. and Lisa Lenard-Cook. *Find Your Story, Write Your Memoir*. University of Wisconsin Press, 2013.

Norton, Lisa Dale. *Shimmering Images: A Handy Little Guide to Writing Memoir.* New York: St. Martin's Griffin, 2008.

Roorbach, Bill. *Writing Life Stories: How to Make Memories into Memoirs, Ideas into Essays, and Life into Literature.* Writer's Digest Books, 2e, 2008.

Silverman, Sue William. *Fearless Confessions: A Writer's Guide to Memoir.* Athens, GA: University of Georgia Press, 2009.

Spence, Linda. *Legacy: A Step-by-Step Guide to Writing Personal History.* Swallow Press, 1997.

Styne, Marlys Marshall. *Seniorwriting: A Brief Guide for Seniors Who Want to Write.* West Conshohocken, PA: Infinity Publishing, 2007.

Traig, Jennifer, ed. *The Autobiographer's Handbook: The 826 National Guide to Writing Your Memoir.* Holt Paperbacks, 2008.

Zinsser, William, ed. *Inventing the Truth: The Art and Craft of Memoir.* Mariner Books, 1998.

Zinsser, William. *Writing about Your Life: A Journey into the Past.* Da Capo Press, 2005.

BOOKS ABOUT ALLSTON-BRIGHTON, ROSLINDALE, SOUTH END, AND WEST ROXBURY

Clarke, Ted. *Brookline, Allston-Brighton and the Renewal of Boston (MA).* The History Press, 2010.

Marchione, William P. *Allston-Brighton, MA (Images of America).* Arcadia Publishing, 1996.

Marchione, William P. *Allston-Brighton in Transition: From Cattle Town to Streetcar Suburb.* The History Press, 2007.

Mishkin, Linda. *Legendary Locals of Allston-Brighton*. Arcadia Publishing, 2013.

Potts, Lynne. *A Block in Time: History of Boston's South End through a Window on Holyoke Street*. Local History Publishers, 2012.

Sammarco, Anthony Mitchell. *Boston's South End (MA) (Then & Now)*. Arcadia Publishing, 2006.

Sammarco, Anthony Mitchell. *Roslindale (MA) (Then & Now)*. Arcadia Publishing, 2003.

Sammarco, Anthony Mitchell. *West Roxbury (MA) (Images of America)*. Arcadia Publishing, 2004.